WHAT PEOPLE ARE SAYING ABOUT OUR BOOKS...

BOOKS OF THE "SECRET" SERIES

California Wine Country Secrets

Monterey's Secrets

San Francisco's Secrets

CALIFORNIA
WINE COUNTRY
SECRETS

Whispered recipes
and guide to
restaurants and
wineries of
Napa/Sonoma

By
Kathleen DeVanna Fish

The Marketing Arm
Monterey, California

Library of Congress Cataloguing-in-Publication Data

CALIFORNIA WINE COUNTRY SECRETS
Whispered Recipes and Guide to Restaurants and Wineries
of Napa/Sonoma.

Fish, Kathleen DeVanna
91-60129
ISBN 0-9620472-4-4
Includes index pages, 267–269
Autobiography page, 271
Copyright 1991
by Kathleen DeVanna Fish

Editor, Fred Hernandez
Cover photography by Robert N. Fish
Cover photo of Joseph Phelps Vineyards
Cover design by Gerald Reis & Company
Back cover, creative design services, Grant Huntington
Photos from Napa County Historical Society, pages 17–19, 213
Photos from the Sonoma Valley
    Historical Society/Depot Museum, pages 81, 83
Photos from Pat Hathaway Collection, pages 5, 150, 211
Type by Electra Typography
Printed by Publishers Press

Published by The Marketing Arm
P.O. Box 1994
Monterey, CA 93942

Printed in the United States of America

INSIDE TIPS

THE ESSENCE OF this book is to let you in on some valuable tips about the Napa and Sonoma areas: from the top chefs' secret recipes to the best restaurants and wineries.

INCLUDED ARE TREASURED recipes from 48 Napa and Sonoma wineries. The 27 hand-picked restaurants go a step further: the award-winning chefs provide full menus and their closely-guarded recipes. You will learn the secrets of such delicacies as Fresh Pumpkin Soup with Minted Cream, Risotto with Smoked Chicken, Caramelized Onions and Walnuts, Swordfish with Wild Mushrooms in Parchment, Lamb grilled with Cabernet Wine Sauce, Polenta Pudding with Fresh Blackberry Compote and Chocolate Decadence Cake. The hundreds of recipes assembled in this collection have been contributed by some of California's most talented chefs. The format is easy to follow, with preparation times ranging from 15 minutes to three hours.

AND, TO HELP YOU get into the spirit of romance and adventure, California Wine Country Secrets is sprinkled with tidbits of history, legend and lore.
Discover the secrets.

NAPA VALLEY RESTAURANTS

NAPA VALLEY WINERIES, 212

SONOMA COUNTY RESTAURANTS

SONOMA COUNTY WINERIES, 240

ALL SEASONS CAFE

Menu for Four   20

PUMPKIN SOUP
WITH MINTED CREAM

SKEWERED SALMON
ON ORIENTAL GREENS

ROASTED QUAIL

AUBERGE DU SOLEIL

Menu for Six   24

SPICY SQUASH SOUP

STEAMED FISH,
GINGER SOYA BEANS

QUINCE TART TATIN

CINNAMON ICE CREAM

BRAVA TERRACE

Menu for Eight   28

DUCK SALAD WITH ARTICHOKES

CASSOULET OF LENTILS

FRESH FRUIT
WITH ENGLISH CREAM

DOMAINE CHANDON

Menu for Six   32

SMOKED RED TROUT FILET

JAPANESE EGGPLANT SOUP

SPICY ROCK SHRIMP RISOTTO

POLENTA PUDDING
WITH COMPOTE

THE FRENCH LAUNDRY

Menu for Four   38

CHILLED AVOCADO SOUP
DUCKLING WITH CURRY GLAZE
APPLE CLAFOUTI
WITH CIDER SAUCE

MUSTARDS GRILL

Menu for Six   42

ROASTED GARLIC
EGGPLANT WITH GINGER BUTTER
GRILLED PORK LOIN,
BLACK BEANS
PICKLED ONIONS,
TOMATILLO SALSA
GINGER AND PEAR CAKE

PIATTI RISTORANTE

Menu for Four   48

GRILLED ITALIAN BREAD
PASTA FANTASIA
TIRAMISU
WITH CRÈME ANGLAISE

RISSA ORIENTAL CAFE

Menu for Four   52

CHICKEN COCONUT SOUP
GYOZA (POTSTICKERS)
THAI SPICY BEEF SALAD

SHOWLEY'S AT MIRAMONTE

Menu for Six   56

SOUTHWEST LASAGNE
TUSCAN BREAD
ROASTED CHINESE GAME HENS
BERRY COBBLER,
CHANTILLY CREAM

STARMONT AT MEADOWOOD

Menu for Four   62

ROAST DUCK WITH HONEY
SHRIMP IN CABBAGE LEAVES
BERRIES, CHAMPAGNE SABAYON

TERRA RESTAURANT

Menu for Six   66

WARM SCALLOP SALAD
GRILLED MEDALLION OF LAMB
STRAWBERRY SHORTCAKE

TRA VIGNE

Menu for Four   70

GRILLED MOZZARELLA
SEAFOOD SOUP
HARVEST FOCCACIA BREAD
FETTUCINE
WITH GRILLED ARTICHOKES

TRILOGY

Menu for Four   76

HALIBUT WITH LEMON GRASS
POLENTA
WITH RED BELL PEPPER SAUCE
WHITE CHOCOLATE MOUSSE
TORTE

BLUE HERON

Menu for Four   84

BAKED BRIE WITH PESTO
LEMON HERB VINAIGRETTE
SWORDFISH
WITH WASABI BUTTER
KAHLUA CHOCOLATE MOUSSE

CAFFE PORTOFINO

Menu for Six   90

PORK WITH BAY LEAVES
AGNOLOTTI PASTA WITH CREAM
AMARETTI-STUFFED PEACHES

CHATEAU SOUVERAIN

Menu for Six   94

CREAM OF ARUGULA SOUP
SQUAB ON SAGE PASTA
RASPBERRY AMARETTO TARTS

DEPOT 1870 RESTAURANT

Menu for Four   100

PRAWNS WITH WHITE BEANS
SPINACH PASTA
CAULIFLOWER SALAD
SCALLOPS OF VEAL
SOUFFLÉ CAKE

WINEMAKERS' FAVORITE RECIPES

STARTERS

Barbecue Chicken Salad, 151
Cheese Sticks, 152
Chevre Soufflé, 153
Goat Cheese Torta, 154
Grilled Leeks with Mustard Cream, 155
Harvest Soup, 156
Leek & Potato Soup with Avocado Cream, 157
Mushroom Strata, 158
Pear & Swiss Cheese Salad, 159
Prosciutto Wild Mushroom Bread, 160
Spinach Balls with Sauvignon Blanc Mustard Sauce, 161
Torta Rustica, 162
Warm Goat Cheese Salad with Golden Pepper Dressing, 163
Wild Rice Salad, 164

PASTA

Smoked Chicken Fettucine with Basil & Pinenuts, 165
Pasta with Shrimp, Asparagus & Cream Sauce, 166
Pasta with Shrimp, & Lemon Butter Sauce, 167
Risotto with Smoked Chicken, Caramelized Onions & Walnuts, 168
Spaghettini Primavera, 169
Roast Turkey with Herb Pasta, 170

MEAT

Barbecue Leg of Lamb, 171
Grilled Rack of Lamb with Cabernet Lamb Sauce, 172
Lamb with Oyster Mushroom Ragout, 173
Merlot Meat Loaf, 174
Barbecue Pork Tenderloin, 175
Grilled Pork Tenderloin, 176
Pork Chops & Apples, 177
Mustard Pepper Steak, 178
Mushroom Veal Stew, 179
Veal Medallions on Spinach with Cabernet Sauvignon Sauce, 180

POULTRY/DUCK

Chicken with Chardonnay & Caper Cream, 181
Chicken Florentine, 182
Chicken stuffed with Swiss Chard, 183
Chicken with Tomatoes & White Wine Sauce, 184
Grilled Tarragon Chicken Skewers, 185
Thai Grilled Chicken, 186
Duck Steak with Shallots, 187
Duck with Pear in Champagne, 188

SEAFOOD

Bay Scallops with Spinach & Pernod, 189
Citrus & Apricot Prawns, 190
Grilled Prawns with Tequila & Nectarine Cream Sauce, 191
Mussels en Croute, 192
Salmon Poached in Champagne & Cream Sauce with Papaya, 193
Salmon with Garlic, Basil & Tomatoes, 194
Salmon with Orange Saffron Butter, 195
Salmon & Sea Bass in Buerre Blanc Sauce, 196
Salmon with Zinfandel Sauce, 197
Swordfish with Wild Mushrooms in Parchment, 198
Tuna with Lavender, 199

DESSERT

Apricot Crown, 200
Fresh Berries with Basil & Mint, 201
Black Currant Tea Ice Cream, 202
Cherry & Chocolate Trifle, 203
Chocolate Decadence Cake, 204
Italian Biscotti, 205
Mousse Grand Cru, 206
Orange Custard with Strawberries & Muscat Canelli, 207
Pears in Port Sauce, 208
Wine Cake with Muscat À Deux, 209
Zabaglione, 210

THE NAPA VALLEY...
HOW IT ALL BEGAN

THERE WAS GOLD, and plenty of it, in California. Between 1850 and 1853, $65 million worth of gold was brought out of the gold-fields each year. Many people got rich as a result of the Gold Rush— and not just those working the fields. People were drawn to the West by the excitement of being a part of the beginning of a new place. And a few of these characters could be classified as eccentric.

Sam Brannan, a renegade Mormon, was the stuff of which legends are made. At the young age of 28, he was California's first millionaire. Sam arrived in San Francisco two years before the Gold Rush and founded the first newspaper, fire department and flour mill. He was also the founder of Calistoga.

Ever the promoter, Sam Brannan looked at the hot springs north of Napa one day and slurred: "It'll be the Calistoga of Sarafornia." And that's how Calistoga got its name.

THE MUD BATHS and geothermal springs of Calistoga were a popular gathering spot for centuries. The Indians quickly learned that the baths eased the pain of arthritis. By common agreement the bath areas were neutral territory, a place of healing. Because of the plumes of steam the Indians had their own name for this place: The land of the smoking earth.

George C. Yount,
a pioneer from
North Carolina,
planted the first
vines in the Napa Valley.

THE NATURAL ALLURE of the baths was not lost on Brannan. He envisioned creating a fashionable spa in Calistoga to rival New York's famed Saratoga. In 1859 he poured half a million dollars into the Springs Ground hotel, a complex of swimming pools, mud baths and a race track for his Arabian horses. Sam persuaded the railroad to extend its track to Calistoga to attract the rich aristocracy of San Francisco. The Charles Crockers and the Leland Stanfords declined, however, leaving Sam Brannan penniless in 1875.

Then there was George Calvert Yount, a pioneer who came west from North Carolina. Yount planted the first vines in the Valley in 1831. It was in Yountville that the first crush took place. Indians danced barefoot on stretched cowhide piled high with grapes before the juice was fermented in skin bags.

Yountville became the wine center, boasting the largest town in the North Valley. Nonetheless, by 1870, Yount was producing only 5,000 gallons of wine a year, while Sam Brannan was distilling 90,000 gallons of brandy at Calistoga. Yountville remained small while the Northern Valley expanded and prospered.

David Doak, a millionaire industrialist, spent millions creating his Georgian-style mansion in Napa only to meet with tragedy there. His home was acquired by the Displaced Carmelites, who transformed it into a monastery. It is ironic that a millionaire's extravagant pleasure palace should end up as the home of men who adhere to a policy of poverty and silence.

A stagecoach in the early days of California

AUTHOR ROBERT LOUIS Stevenson arrived in Calistoga in May 1880. Having just married Fannie Osborne, he brought her to Calistoga for their honeymoon. For three rent-free months they stayed in a miner's ramshackle cabin, where he worked on a series of sketches entitled "Silverado Squatters."

"We are in a land of stage drivers and highwaymen," Stevenson wrote, about drivers like Clark Foss, "who could handle six horses like so many cats, and was more of an attraction than the geyser." Stevenson also wrote of "Petrified Charlie", who uncovered the famous Petrified Forest west of Calistoga while clearing a field.

AND FINALLY, THE European winemakers began to arrive, beginning with the Germans. Charles Krug, a Prussian emigrant founded the first commercial winery in Napa Valley in 1861 and now the oldest operating winery. In 1862, Jacob Schram planted his vines to establish Schramsberg. The Beringer brothers, Jacob and Frederick followed with winemaking techniques learned in the Medoc.

By 1880, winemaking was the major occupation of the Valley.

THE ETHNIC and cultural heritage of the Valley is rich with German, French and Italian influences as well as the Chinese, who came into California during the Gold Rush. Many of the stone bridges and wineries in the Valley were built by the Chinese. They also painstakingly excavated the tunnels of sandstone with pick and shovel for Beringer, Schramsberg and Stags' Leap Wineries.

The Silverado Trail, along the eastern edge of the Valley, was the original route from the Cinnabar Mines of Mt. St. Helena to the loading dock on San Pablo Bay. Massive ore wagons, pulled by oxen, dragged large loads to the water's edge. Today, its greatest value is the scenic beauty of the trail and the welcome relief from the traffic of Highway 29.

THE RICH HERITAGE of Napa Valley wines led inevitably to extraordinary food. The fertile soil produced a lavish bounty of crops.

The combination of fine wines and fine ingredients survive to this day in the abundant tastes of Napa Valley

The Gold Rush saw a large influx of Chinese into the Napa Valley.

ALL SEASONS CAFE & WINE SHOP

MEDITERRANEAN CUISINE
1400 Lincoln Avenue
Calistoga
942-9111
Lunch, Thursday–Tuesday 11:30AM–4PM
Dinner, Thursday–Monday 5PM–10PM
AVERAGE DINNER FOR TWO: $48

ALL SEASONS IS a sunny corner cafe whose marble-topped tables and checkered tile floor contribute to a casual brasserie atmosphere.

The seasonally changing menus draw inspiration from the wealth of North Coast-grown products which are assembled into dishes with overtones of Mediterranean, Southwest and Asian cuisines. The pastry chefs make all desserts and breads, plus exceptional croissants, scones and biscotti to be enjoyed with an espresso or cappuccino. The homemade ice cream features flavors from ginger to raspberry chocolate chip.

The courses are arranged to complement the many fine wines featured by the glass, as well as the hundreds of wines on the master wine list. The restaurant's extremely fair pricing policy for wines makes even the most rare and older wines excellent values. The wine shop has one of the most extensive collections of hard to find boutique wines from California as well as an outstanding collection of the best of Burgundy.

ALL SEASONS
CAFE & WINE SHOP

Chef Mark Dierkhising's Menu for Four

Pumpkin Soup with Minted Cream
Skewered Salmon on Oriental Greens with Soy Dressing
Roasted Quail with Cabernet Essence

Pumpkin Soup with Minted Cream

Copyright M. Dierkhising

Serves 4
Preparation Time: 2 Hours
Pre-heat oven to 400°

8 lbs. fresh pumpkin	4 Tbsps. unsalted butter
2 lbs. butternut squash	1 qt. chicken stock
2 medium onions, diced	2 cups heavy cream
2 carrots, diced	Salt and pepper to taste
2 garlic cloves	

Roast the pumpkin and squash whole, in a 400° oven for 30–45 minutes or until soft. Remove from oven and cool.

In a large soup pot, place onions, carrots and whole garlic cloves with the unsalted butter. Cook until onions are soft and transparent. Add chicken stock and continue to cook.

Remove the skins and seeds from the pumpkin and squash and dice. Add to the soup and continue cooking until pumpkin and squash are soft and incorporated into the stock mixture. Add cream and bring to a boil. Remove from heat and purée in a blender. Return to a clean pot, season with salt and pepper. Heat thoroughly. Serve with garnish of Minted Cream.

Minted Cream

20 mint leaves	**1 cup heavy cream**

Place the mint leaves in a quart of boiling water for a count of ten. Drain and chill leaves in an ice water bath. Remove and pat dry. Place the leaves and cream into a blender. Purée until well incorporated. Strain the cream mixture and use the mint cream to garnish the pumpkin soup.

Skewered Salmon on Oriental Greens

Copyright M. Dierkhising

Serves 4
Preparation Time: 30 Minutes

8 three-ounce strips of salmon
2 One-inch pieces fresh ginger
4 Tbsps. Indonesian Ketjap (available in specialty stores)
4 Tbsps. sesame oil
4 garlic cloves, chopped
8 eight-inch bamboo skewers
2 bunches Red Mustard or other Oriental greens
2 Tbsps. sesame seeds

Place salmon into a glass or stainless steel pan. Smash each piece of ginger with a heavy cleaver to release some of the juices. Using your hands, squeeze the ginger juice onto the salmon pieces. Sprinkle the garlic over the salmon.

In a separate bowl, combine the sesame oil and Indonesian Ketjap. Pour over the salmon strips. Marinate for at least 15 minutes to 24 hours.

Gently push the salmon strips onto the bamboo skewers, leaving a small handle on each end. Grill for 4–5 minutes on each side or until done.

Toss the greens with the soy dressing (recipe follows) and divide equally among four plates. Place the salmon strips on top of the greens and sprinkle with sesame seeds.

Soy Dressing

4 Tbsps. soy sauce
4 Tbsps. sesame oil
4 Tbsps. orange juice
2 sweet oranges, peeled, sectioned

Prepare the dressing by whisking together the soy sauce, sesame oil and orange juice. Add the orange sections into the dressing and blend.

Roasted Quail
with Cabernet Essence

Copyright M. Dierkhising

Serves 4 (2 quails per person)
Preparation Time: 1½ Hours
Pre-heat oven to 375°

8 whole quails
2 Tbsps. butter
1 medium onion, chopped
2 carrots, chopped
2 stalks celery, chopped
1 bottle Cabernet Sauvignon
4 whole black peppercorns
4 Tbsps. shallots, chopped
4 Tbsps. parsley, chopped
1 cup chicken stock

Clean quails under cold running water. Pat dry with towel and set aside.

Rub softened butter onto the bottom of a roasting pan. Place diced vegetables into pan. Lay 8 quails on top of vegetables and roast at 375° for 20–30 minutes. Remove from oven and keep warm.

Prepare the sauce by combining the Cabernet Sauvignon, peppercorns, shallots and parsley into a sauce pan. Reduce over medium heat to one half cup. Add the chicken stock a little at a time until you achieve the flavors you like. Strain and reserve for the roasted quail.

AUBERGE DU SOLEIL

CALIFORNIA COUNTRY CUISINE
180 Rutherford Hill Road
Rutherford
963-1211
Lunch daily 11AM–2PM
Dinner 6PM–9PM
AVERAGE DINNER FOR TWO: $120

THE AUBERGE DU SOLEIL RESORT is nestled in a 33-acre hillside olive grove overlooking the Napa Valley. This unique hide-away, composed of private maisons, restaurant and recreational facilities, has been designed to portray the informal but elegant tradition of the finest European country inns. Simple, peaceful, grand and intimate best describe the main building that houses the famous Auberge du Soleil Restaurant.

Relax on the terrace for lunch or dress for dinner and experience elegant California dining. In this lighthearted atmosphere, savor favored chef's specials such as potato pancakes with salmon and golden caviar in champagne sauce or bay scallops with tomatillo and corn salsa. Tempting desserts of walnut cheesecake smothered in bitter-sweet chocolate sauce with persimmons or poached butter pears in Cabernet Sauvignon with cinnamon ice cream are fine examples of the alluring dinner cuisine offered by Chef Udo Nechutny.

Chef Udo Nechutny's Menu for Six

Spicy Squash Soup
Steamed Fish with Cabbage, Shiitake Mushrooms,
Ginger Soya Beans
Quince Tart Tatin with Cinnamon Ice Cream

Spicy Squash Soup

Serves 6
Preparation Time: 45 Minutes
Pre-heat oven to 350°

2 butternut squash
2 yellow onions
1 mild chile pepper
1 Tbsp. butter
1 qt. chicken stock
1 Tbsp. whole cumin seeds
Whipped cream garnish
1 cup pine nuts
Salt and pepper to taste

Cut squash in half and discard pulp. Place face down in roasting pan with enough water to coat the bottom. Bake at 350° until soft. Remove from oven and peel off skin.

Sauté the onions and chile pepper in butter over low heat. When onions are transparent, add the cooked squash and any remaining juices from the squash pan. Add the chicken stock and bring to simmer.

Toast cumin seeds in hot dry pan until golden brown. Remove and grind to a fine powder. Add to the soup with the salt and pepper to taste.

Garnish with a dollop of lightly whipped cream and toasted pine nuts.

Steamed Fish with Cabbage, Shiitake Mushrooms and Ginger Soya Beans

Serves 6
Preparation Time: 30 Minutes

1 head Tinsin (Napa) cabbage
6 portions halibut or other flat fish
1 cup shiitake mushrooms, quartered
4 Tbsps. olive oil
4 Tbsps. shallots, chopped
2 Tbsps. ginger, grated
2 garlic cloves, chopped
2 Tbsps. black fermented soya beans
2 Tbsps. scallions, chopped
   Cilantro for garnish
   Parchment paper

On six individual sheets of parchment paper, place cabbage leaves with the fish on top. Top fish with mushrooms. Fold the parchment paper and steam over boiling water until fish is cooked. Remove fish from parchment and place on individual plates.

In a sauté pan, heat olive oil and add shallots, garlic, ginger and black beans. When sauce is hot, drizzle over and around fish.

Garnish with sliced scallions and cilantro.

Cooking tip: Black fermented soya beans are available in Chinese or specialty stores.

Quince Tart Tatin

Serves 6
Preparation Time: One hour (note refrigeration time)
Pre-heat oven to 325°

½ cup sugar	3 egg yolks
1¼ cups flour	Pinch of salt
8 Tbsps. butter	6 ripe quinces

In a large mixing bowl, blend sugar and flour. Cut butter into slices and mix until well blended. Add egg yolks and salt, pressing dough mixture together. Avoid over-mixing. Refrigerate pastry dough at least one hour.

On a sheet pan, place six dollops of butter and a pinch of sugar. Peel quince and slice each in half, scooping out seeds. Top each butter dollop with the quince, cut side up. Press down to slightly fan. Place another small dollop of butter on top of quince and sprinkle with sugar. Bake at 325° until cooked but firm, approximately 30 minutes.

Roll out sweet pastry to ¼" thick and cut out circles a little larger than the quince halves. Prick with a fork and bake until golden brown, about 8–10 minutes.

Top pastry with quince and sprinkle with sugar. Caramelize with a hot iron or under the broiler. Serve with cinnamon ice cream.

Cinnamon Ice Cream

Serves 6
Preparation Time: 45 Minutes

1 pt. half and half	1 slice lemon peel
1 pt. heavy cream	12 egg yolks
1 vanilla bean, sliced in half	¾ cup sugar
6 cinnamon sticks	

Steep half and half, heavy cream, vanilla bean, cinnamon stick and lemon peel for 15 minutes.

Lightly beat yolks and add sugar. Add cream mixture and cook over medium heat until thick, stirring constantly. Strain and cool before freezing.

BRAVA TERRACE

MEDITERRANEAN CUISINE
3010 St. Helena Highway
St. Helena
963-9300
Lunch & Dinner 11:30AM–9PM
Closed Monday
AVERAGE DINNER FOR TWO: $60

"CUISINES OF THE SUN" is the name Chef Fred Halpert bestows upon the menu inspired by the collective wine country cooking of France, Italy and California for his new Brava Terrace restaurant. He has created a light style that relies heavily on seafood, olive oil, garlic, tomatoes and fresh herbs. Provençal cooking does not mask the flavors and opens up great possibilities for matching food with the abundant flavors of Napa Valley wines.

As the name implies, Brava Terrace has an outdoor patio dining area that overlooks the lush vineyards of the valley. Inside, the dining area is light and airy, and an open kitchen enables patrons to watch Halpert work his magic.

The menu features several grilled entrées, fresh seafood and Provençal favorites like Cassoulet. Halpert's wine list reflects his love of California wines and runs the gamut of varietals.

Brava Terrace is run by people who love to cook for people who love to eat.

Duck Salad
with Artichokes & Mixed Greens

Serves 8
Preparation Time: 30 Minutes

2 **artichokes**
1 **lemon**
2 **duck breasts**
2 **Tbsps. olive oil**
   Assorted lettuce: green leaf, red leaf, etc.
¼ **cup walnut oil**
½ **Tbsp. balsamic vinegar**
½ **Tbsp. lemon juice**
   White pepper
   Chives, chopped
   Chervil, chopped

Clean artichokes and poach in lemon water until cooked. Cut out the heart of the artichoke and slice. Set aside.

Sauté duck breast in olive oil and cook to medium rare. Slice duck breasts and set aside.

Prepare vinaigrette by mixing walnut oil, vinegar and lemon juice together. Season with white pepper.

Toss salad with vinaigrette and arrange duck and artichoke slices around the salad. Sprinkle with chives and chervil before serving.

Cassoulet of Lentils with Lamb, Sausage & Pork

Serves 8
Preparation Time: 45 Minutes

      1 carrot, diced
      1 medium onion, diced
      2 celery stalks, diced
    ¼ cup olive oil
      2 cups lentils
      1 bay leaf
      2 thyme sprigs
   1¼ cups chicken stock
      1 lb. pork loin
      1 lb. leg of lamb, trimmed
         Salt and white pepper to taste
      1 lb. link sausages
      1 lb. mushrooms, quartered
      2 Tbsps. unsalted butter
      1 bunch chives, chopped

Sauté carrots, onion and celery with olive oil over medium heat. Add lentils, bay leaf and thyme and sauté 1 minute. Add chicken stock and bring to a boil. Cover and cook for 15 minutes on medium heat or until lentils are al dente, stirring occasionally. Remove from heat.

Cut the pork loin and lamb in half. Season with salt and pepper. Sear until rare. Remove from pan and quarter lamb and pork pieces.

Cut sausages in half and sear over high heat. Remove from heat and set aside.

Sauté mushrooms separately with butter.

Return lentils to heat. Add all ingredients to lentils and cook until meats reach desired doneness. (2 minutes rare, 4 minutes medium, 6 minutes well-done). Season to taste.

Portion into 8 individual serving bowls and garnish with chives.

Cooking tip: Try duck, venison or specialty game sausages for variation.

Fresh Fruit
with English Cream & Mint

Serves 8
Preparation Time: 25 Minutes

1½ **vanilla beans**
  1 **qt. milk**
  8 **egg yolks**
  ¾ **cup sugar**
    Assorted seasonal fruit, sliced
    Mint leaves, julienned

Split vanilla beans in half. Scrape seeds. Add to milk and boil over medium heat. Remove from heat.

In a mixing bowl blend egg yolks and sugar until color is light. Add ⅓ of the boiled milk to the egg mixture. Mix thoroughly.

Add the egg mixture to the remaining ⅔ of the milk and return to heat, boiling for 1 minute. Strain and cool.

Place mixed fruit in serving bowl and drizzle with sauce. Sprinkle with mint and serve.

DOMAINE CHANDON

CALIFORNIA & FRENCH CUISINE
1 California Drive
Yountville
944-2892
May–October, Wednesday–Sunday
Lunch daily 11:30AM–2:30PM
Dinner 6PM–9PM
May–November lunch open daily
AVERAGE DINNER FOR TWO: $65

DOMAINE CHANDON'S RESTAURANT is intended to showcase its sparkling wines. The menu is carefully designed to enhance the wines, using to full advantage the wealth of fresh ingredients available in California, as well as the versatility of sparkling wine with food.

Philippe Jeanty, chef de cuisine, and a native of Champagne, began his career under the famed Joseph Thuet, Maître Cuisinier de France, at Moët et Chandon.

Jeanty is well know for his innovative but simple style of cooking, based on classic country cuisine. As a result, patrons are likely to encounter Spicy Florida Rock Shrimp Risotto, Home-Smoked Red Trout with a Crispy Potato Salad, Tomato Soup in Puff Pastry, Espresso and Mascarpone Ice Cream Sandwich with a Crunchy Peanut Butter layer and Bittersweet Chocolate Sauce.

Interesting food can be made even more exciting when served with sparkling wine. Domaine Chandon's Restaurant is a place for unhurried dining and quiet conversation in an intimate atmosphere.

Chef Philippe Jeanty's Menu for Six

Smoked Red Trout Filet on Crisp Potato Salad
Japanese Eggplant Soup with
Goat's Milk Mozzarella Croutons
Spicy Florida Rock Shrimp Risotto
Polenta Pudding with Fresh Blackberry Compote
& Mascarpone Whipped Cream

Smoked Red Trout Filet on Crisp Potato Salad

Serves 8
Preparation Time: 1½ Hours (note marinating time)

 4 **baby trout filets, ½ lb. each**
 3 **cups olive oil**
 8 **bay leaves**
 ⅓ **cup whole black peppercorns**
16 **sprigs fresh thyme**
 1 **large onion, sliced thin**
 1 **large carrot, sliced paper thin**
 2 **large baking potatoes**
 1 **head frisee lettuce**
 1 **Belgian endive or red oak leaf lettuce**
   Chervil for garnish
   Black pepper to taste
   Balsamic vinegar

Marinate the trout filets overnight with the skin left on, in olive oil with bay leaves, peppercorns, thyme, onion and carrot.

Bake unpeeled washed potatoes at 400° for 45 minutes. Cut in half widthwise, then into 4 wedges each. Set aside.

Arrange frisee and endive on plate with carrot slices from marinade. Reheat potato wedges, then toss lightly in the oil from the marinade. Slice each trout into 3 pieces and arrange over potato. Drape onion over trout and garnish with chervil and cracked pepper. Drizzle oil and balsamic vinegar over salad and serve.

Japanese Eggplant Soup with Goat's Milk Mozzarella Croutons

Serves 6
Preparation Time: 1 Hour
Pre-heat oven to 400°

1½ lbs. Japanese eggplant
2 medium yellow onions
1 medium red pepper
3 Roma tomatoes
8 cloves garlic, peeled
3 sprigs thyme, chopped

3 sprigs basil, chopped
1 bay leaf, crumbled
1 Tbsp. unsalted butter
½ cup extra virgin olive oil
2 qts. chicken stock
  Salt and pepper to taste

Halve the eggplant, lightly coat with olive oil, salt and pepper. Halve the onions lengthwise, cut out the root end and peel down to the last layer of skin. Halve the pepper, remove stem and seed, lightly coat with olive oil and salt and pepper. Remove stem end from the tomatoes.

Place all these ingredients on a foil-lined sheet pan. Skin side down for the eggplant, cut side down for the onion, skin side up for the pepper.

Place in 400° oven until the eggplant and pepper brown, 20–25 minutes. After about 10 minutes, add the garlic cloves next to the tomatoes to prevent the garlic from burning.

When the eggplant is roasted and the pepper halves are brown and puffy, remove pan from oven. Cool and peel the onion and the pepper. Coarsely chop the eggplant, pepper, onion and garlic.

In an 8 qt. pot, melt the butter and add the remaining olive oil. Add the chopped vegetables and herbs. Mix well. Add enough chicken stock to barely cover. Bring to a boil and add the bay leaf. Let the soup simmer until it starts to thicken.

Purée in a blender until thick and textured and flecked with the black bits of eggplant.

When serving, add chicken stock to base until it has a stew-like consistency. Salt and pepper to taste. Top each portion with Goats' Milk Mozzarella Croutons. (Toasted sliced bread with a ¼″ slice of mozzarella on top, melted in the oven.)

Spicy Florida Rock Shrimp Risotto

Serves 6
Preparation Time: 45 Minutes

1½ lbs. Florida Rock shrimp, peeled, deveined
3 Tbsps. olive oil
½ medium yellow onion, chopped
1 lb. risotto (Arborio rice)
4 leaves fresh sage
2 sprigs fresh thyme
2 qts. chicken stock
¾ cup tomato purée
   Salt and cayenne pepper to taste
4 Tbsps. Parmesan cheese, grated
1½ oz. pancetta, julienned
1 sprig fresh basil, julienned leaves
2 Tbsps. fresh parsley, chopped
6 Tbsps. sweet butter

In a large stock pot, heat olive oil over medium high heat. Add onions, cook for 3 minutes, stirring with a wooden spatula so the onions do not color. Add risotto, sage and thyme, cooking for 2 minutes, while stirring. Add boiling chicken stock slowly to the risotto and cook for 10 minutes or until al dente.

Add shrimp, tomato, cayenne pepper, Parmesan and pancetta. Continue to cook while stirring, until risotto is creamy. Finish by adding basil, parsley and sweet butter.

To serve, divide into 6 soup plates.

Cooking tip: This risotto should have the sweetness of the shrimp, a little of the heat from the cayenne pepper and the freshness of the basil.

Polenta Pudding
with Fresh Blackberry Compote
and Mascarpone Whipped Cream

Serves 8
Preparation Time: 2 Hours (note refrigeration time)
Pre-heat oven to 325°

1½ cups sweet butter
  5 cups powdered sugar
 ¼ vanilla bean, scraped inside
  4 eggs
  2 egg yolks
  2 cups bread flour
  1 cup polenta
    Mint garnish

In an electric mixer, beat the butter, sugar and vanilla bean until creamy. Beat in the eggs and egg yolks one at a time. Fold in flour and polenta.

Pour into 12" greased and floured cake pan. Bake 1 hour, 15 minutes at 325.°

Unmold on a rack and let cool.

Place cake in a larger size cake pan. Pour cooked berries and juices on top and around cake, cover and soak overnight. (berry compote recipe follows)

Cut cake into slices and garnish with mascarpone cream (recipe follows) and a few fresh blackberries. Add a few drops of Petite Liqueur, a mint tip and some of the berry juices around the cake.

Serve at room temperature.

Berry Compote

4 cups fresh blackberries
½ cup sugar
¼ cup Petite Liqueur

Cook the blackberries, sugar and Petite Liqueur over low heat for 10 minutes. Reserve a few berries for garnish.

Mascarpone Whipped Cream

½ cup mascarpone
1 cup whipping cream
3 Tbsps. sugar

In a mixing bowl, combine the mascarpone, whipping cream and sugar. Whip to a soft peak.

THE FRENCH LAUNDRY

CONTEMPORARY FRENCH CUISINE
Washington and Creek Streets
Yountville
944-2380
One dinner seating beginning at 7PM
Wednesday through Sunday
AVERAGE DINNER FOR TWO: $92

THE FRENCH LAUNDRY is housed in a charming old stone, two-story residence, which served as a laundry for 40 years. The restaurant is surrounded by trees, flowers and herb gardens, which you are encouraged to enjoy between dinner courses. Owners Don and Sally Schmidt built their high-quality restaurant around superb food in a relaxed and inviting atmosphere.

The fixed menu changes nightly, offering some choices of appetizers and desserts. The prix fixe dinner of $46 features five courses and coffee.

Sally Schmidt presides in the kitchen, offering simple but beautifully prepared dishes such as summer tomatoes with arugula mayonnaise, crispy duck with homemade chutney and mustard and a shortcake of nectarines and red berries.

The French Laundry is a place for unhurried dining, expert service, wonderful local wines and outstanding food.

THE FRENCH LAUNDRY

Chef Sally Schmidt's Menu for Four

Chilled Avocado Soup
Duckling with a Curry Glaze
Apple Clafouti with Cider Sauce

Chilled Avocado Soup

Serves 4
Preparation Time: 20 Minutes

4 ripe avocados, peeled
¼ cup lime juice
1 cup chicken stock
2 cups buttermilk
1 cup light cream
½ cup white onion, minced fine
   Fresh black pepper, coarsely ground
   Chives for garnish

   In a large mixing bowl, mash avocados, add lime juice, then the other ingredients. Whisk until smooth, then to consistency of thick cream using extra stock or milk if needed. Taste for seasoning. Use plenty of black pepper. Chill.
   Garnish each bowl with chopped chives, including the chive blossom.

Cooking tip: The soup can be made several hours in advance. The lime juice keeps it from darkening.

Duckling with a Curry Glaze

Serves 4
Preparation Time: 3½ hours

Two 5 lb. ducks
2 onions, minced
2 Tbsps. fresh ginger, minced
   Parsley sprigs
   Black peppercorns
4 cloves garlic, sliced
2 Tbsps. curry powder
4 cups duck stock
   Salt to taste
   Squeeze of lime

Bone the duck into 4 pieces, leg and thigh (2) and the breast with wing connections (2). Use bones and giblets, excluding liver, to make a stock.

Cover the bones and giblets with water, at least 2 qts., and add 1 onion, 1 Tbsp. ginger, parsley sprigs and black peppercorns. Simmer at least 2 hours. Strain and skim fat. This should yield at least 1 qt. of stock.

Place duck, skin side up, on a baking sheet with sides, and bake uncovered at 400° for 1 to 1½ hours, basting with the fat that accumulates, until very brown. Remove from oven and pour off fat.

Sauté the remaining onion, garlic and ginger in a little of the duck fat. Add curry powder and cook for a few minutes. Add the duck stock and let simmer until needed. Salt to taste.

Drizzle 1 cup of the curry stock over the duck pieces. Cover loosely with foil and return to the oven at 250° for another 1½ hours. This will return moisture to the duck and will tenderize it. Remove foil from top of duck and let crisp for 30 minutes.

Finish the curry glaze by skimming off any fat. Whirl in blender until smooth. Reheat and add a squeeze of lime to sharpen the flavor.

To serve, spoon glaze over each duck piece. May be served with apricot chutney.

Cooking tip: Accompany with Basmati rice and baby bok choy sautéed with sliced shiitake mushrooms.

Apple Clafouti with Cider Sauce

Serves 4
Preparation Time: 45 Minutes
Pre-heat oven to 375°

  6 **cups gravenstein or golden delicious apples**
¼ **cup butter**
¾ **cup sugar**
  3 **Tbsps. brandy**
  3 **eggs**
  1 **cup light cream**
  1 **tsp. vanilla**
  3 **Tbsps. butter, melted**
⅔ **cup flour**
  1 **Tbsp. cinnamon**

Peel and slice apples. Melt butter in sauté pan and add apples, ¼ cup sugar and brandy. Stir and cook gently until just cooked through. Set aside.

In the blender, make the batter by combining ½ cup sugar, eggs, cream, vanilla, butter and flour. Set aside.

Put a large 10″ pie plate in a 375° oven to get hot. Brush hot pie plate with butter. Pour in half the batter. Add apples, saving a spoonful for the top. Add remaining batter. Top batter with apple and any juices. Sprinkle with sugar and cinnamon.

Bake 25–30 minutes or just until set. Serve hot or cold with a little heavy cream and/or cider sauce.

Cider Sauce

Reduce 2 quarts. of good apple juice or cider by letting boil rapidly in a wide pan until it is slightly thick or it coats a spoon. This amount will yield about 1 cup when reduced enough. It will thicken more when it cools. Spoon over each serving, on top of the cream if used.

MUSTARDS GRILL

AMERICAN CUISINE
7399 St. Helena Hwy.
Yountville
944-2424
Daily 11:30AM–10PM
Full bar
AVERAGE DINNER FOR TWO: $40

SURROUNDED BY VINEYARDS, this small country grill has warmth and character that appeals to both local clientele and visitors. There is a garden on the south side of the restaurant and much of the produce found on the menu gets its start here. A small patio with tables at the entrance is a perfect spot to watch the "who's who" of the Napa Valley discuss the coming grape harvest.

Once inside, Mustards Grill's lively atmosphere stimulates the appetite. "Bright flavors" is a term often used to characterize the food. The oakwood smoker fills the restaurant with aromas of barbecued baby back ribs and smoked quail. The woodburning grill also produces its share of dishes that grace Mustards Grill's memorable menu.

G · R · I · L · L

Roasted Garlic

Serves 6
Preparation Time: 1 Hour
Pre-heat oven to 300°

6 heads of garlic
  Olive oil
  Coarse salt, optional
  Fresh thyme, optional
  Freshly ground pepper, optional
  Unsalted butter, melted
  Sourdough baguette, sliced

Cut each head of garlic half way down from top to expose tops of each clove. Place cloves on a pan where they can fit together quite tightly. Drizzle each bulb liberally with olive oil. If desired, sprinkle a little salt directly onto cloves, but not onto oil between them. Sprinkle fresh pepper and fresh thyme directly onto garlic, too, if desired.

Cover pan with foil. Bake at 300° for 1 hour or more, or until just tender.

Remove from oven and spread the soft, roasted garlic on the sourdough baguette and serve.

43

Eggplant with Ginger Butter

Serves 6
Preparation Time: 15 Minutes

    6 Japanese eggplants, medium sized
      Virgin olive oil
    3 red onions, peeled, sliced into rounds
   10 Tbsps. (1¼ sticks) unsalted butter, sliced
      1-inch piece ginger root, peeled, grated
    1 shallot, peeled, minced
   ¼ tsp. salt
      Ground white pepper to taste

Slice eggplants lengthwise almost to the core several times, so they fan out. Brush with olive oil and grill over hot coals, 3 minutes per side. Brush onion slices with oil and grill at the same time. Set aside.

Prepare the ginger butter by combining the butter, ginger root, shallot, salt and white pepper in a food processor. Mix well.

To serve, fan eggplants out on plates, inserting a slice of onion between each slice of eggplant. Top with ginger butter.

Grilled Pork Loin with Black Beans

Serves 6
Preparation Time: 1½ Hours (note soaking time)

1 lb. black beans	1 tsp. cayenne
4½ cups water	¾ tsp. freshly ground
¼ lb. bacon, chopped	white pepper
5 medium cloves garlic, peeled, minced	2 qts. chicken stock or canned chicken broth
2 stalks celery, minced	1 cup mesquite chips
1 carrot, peeled, diced	One 4 lb. pork loin,
1 onion, peeled, diced	boned, cut into ¾" slices
1 jalapeño chile pepper, seeded, minced	Pickled onions (recipe follows)
1 bay leaf	Tomatillo Salsa
1 Tbsp. chile powder	(recipe follows)
1 tsp. ground cumin	

Soak beans in water for 24 hours. Drain. Transfer to a large saucepan and cover with a generous amount of cold water. Boil for 20 minutes. Drain. Rinse beans and drain again.

In a large, heavy saucepan, cook bacon until golden brown and crisp, stirring frequently, about 5 minutes. Add garlic, celery, carrot, onion, jalapeño and bay leaf. Cook until vegetables are tender, stirring occasionally, about 10 minutes. Add chile powder, cumin, cayenne and white pepper. Stir until aromatic, about 1 minute. Add beans and stock. Simmer, stirring occasionally, until beans are tender and most of the liquid is absorbed, about 1½ hours. Season to taste with salt.

Build a wood or charcoal fire. Soak mesquite chips in water for 30 minutes and drain. Place pork slices between sheets of waxed paper. Using a mallet or the flat side of a cleaver, pound to a thickness of ½." Sprinkle pork with salt and pepper to taste. Grease grill rack. Sprinkle coals with mesquite chips. Arrange pork on grill rack and cook until springy to touch, about 3 minutes per side.

Arrange pork in center of plates. Spoon with salsa on top. Mound pickled onions on one side of pork and black beans on the other.

Pickled Onions

Serves 6
Preparation Time: 25 Minutes

½ cup olive oil
2 lbs. white onions,
   cut into wedges
1½ cups sugar
1 cup red wine vinegar

¼ cup tomato ketchup
2 Tbsps. sea salt
2 tsps. dried red chile flakes
   Freshly ground
   white pepper

Heat oil in a large, heavy saucepan over low heat. Add onions and mix well. Cover and cook until tender, stirring occasionally, about 15 minutes.

Add remaining ingredients and simmer for 3 minutes. Serve warm or at room temperature.

Tomatillo Salsa

Serves 6
Preparation Time: 25 Minutes

½ jalapeño pepper, seeded,
   chopped
¾ lb. tomatillos, peeled
½ cup scallions, minced
¼ cup parsley, minced
2 Tbsps. olive oil
2 Tbsps. lime juice

3 garlic cloves, peeled,
   minced
1 tsp. grated lime zest
¼ tsp. salt
¼ tsp. freshly ground
   white pepper

Char the jalapeño over gas flame or under broiler until skin is blackened and blistered, about 3 minutes. Remove from flame and enclose in a paper bag and steam for 10 minutes. Remove skin and discard seeds. Rinse and pat dry.

Blanch tomatillos in boiling salted water for 3 minutes. Drain. Rinse under cold, running water and drain thoroughly. Transfer to a food processor or blender. Add chile and remaining ingredients. Purée until smooth.

Ginger and Pear Cake

Serves 6
Preparation Time: 1 Hour
Pre-heat oven to 375°

   5 **Tbsps. unsalted butter**
  ⅔ **cup sugar**
   1 **large egg**
  ¾ **cup molasses**
   2 **cups cake flour**
   1 **tsp. baking soda**
  ½ **tsp. salt**
   2 **Tbsps. ginger root, peeled, grated**
   2 **pears, peeled, cored, grated**
   1 **cup low-fat milk**

Butter and flour a 9″ square cake pan. Set aside.

Cream butter and sugar together until light and smooth. Beat in egg. Add molasses, stirring until smooth.

Sift the flour, baking soda and salt together and add to the butter mixture.

In a separate bowl, combine the ginger root, pears and milk. Slowly add to the batter.

Pour batter into prepared cake pan. Bake until center springs back to a light touch, about 45 minutes at 375.° Cool on a rack before serving.

PIATTI RISTORANTE

ITALIAN CUISINE
6480 Washington Street
Yountville
944-2070
Monday–Friday lunch 11:30AM–2:30PM
Dinner 5PM–10PM
Saturday–Sunday 12 Noon–10PM
AVERAGE DINNER FOR TWO: $25

SINCE ITS FOUNDING in 1987, Ristorante Piatti has become one of the restaurant business' shining success stories. From one restaurant, Piatti has grown to five restaurants, with more on the way. The casual atmosphere and traditional regional Italian cuisine draws diners from every point of the globe.

The open kitchen, wood-burning oven, red-tiled floor, big windows and white pine furnishings provide the right ambience for the menu. Piatti is an authentic Italian restaurant, as friendly and inviting as a neighborhood trattoria.

Bon appétit!

RISTORANTE PIATTI

Grilled Italian Bread (Bruschetta)

Serves 4
Preparation Time: 15 Minutes

 1 **tsp. garlic, chopped**
 1 **cup olive oil**
 8 **ripe Roma tomatoes, diced**
20 **fresh basil leaves, julienned**
 1 **tsp. oregano**
   Salt and pepper to taste
 1 **garlic bulb**
12 **slices thick crusty Italian bread**
   Black olives for garnish

In a mixing bowl, combine the chopped garlic, ½ cup olive oil, tomatoes, basil and oregano. Salt and pepper to taste. Let mixture stand for 30 minutes at room temperature.

Cut garlic bulb in half and rub each slice of bread on both sides. Brush lightly with remaining olive oil.

Toast in oven with broiler, turning slices when golden brown and finish other side the same way.

Place slices on a large platter and top with tomato mixture evenly. Garnish with olives and serve.

Pasta Fantasia

Serves 4
Preparation Time: 15 Minutes

 4 Tbsps. olive oil
28 large shrimp, peeled, deveined
 3 cloves garlic, finely chopped
½ tsp. chile flakes
 1 lb. fresh papardelle or fettucine pasta
 2 Tbsps. Italian parsley, chopped
   Salt and fresh ground black pepper to taste
   Juice of 1 lemon
10 Tbsps. (1¼ sticks) butter
 4 large Roma tomatoes, seeded, diced
 2 bunches arugula, stems removed

Bring a large pot of salted water to a boil.

In a large skillet, heat olive oil, adding the shrimp, garlic and chile flakes. Cook over medium heat for about 3 minutes.

Add pasta to water. Fresh pasta will cook in about 3 to 4 minutes. If you use dry pasta, start boiling your pasta before you start cooking the shrimp.

Add parsley, salt and fresh ground pepper to the sautéed shrimp. Stir in lemon juice and butter.

Drain pasta and add to the shrimp. Toss in tomatoes and arugula. Check the seasoning and adjust if necessary. Serve immediately.

Tiramisu

Serves 4
Preparation Time: 30 Minutes (note refrigeration time)

 3 **egg yolks**
 1 **cup mascarpone cheese**
¼ **cup sugar**
½ **cup cream, whipped**
 1 **box lady fingers (about 50 pieces)**
 7 **cups espresso or strong coffee**
½ **cup dark rum**
   Ground chocolate

In a mixer, beat eggs, mascarpone and sugar until fluffy and creamy. Fold in whipped cream. Set aside.

Combine the coffee and rum. Dip each lady finger in the coffee rum mixture, sugar side down, for 1 second. Lady fingers get soggy very quickly.

Layer lady fingers in a 3″ deep rectangular pan. Cover with mascarpone mixture. Repeat procedure until all the mascarpone and lady fingers are used. Chill for 2 hours.

Garnish with ground chocolate and crème anglaise.

Crème Anglaise

 7 **egg yolks**
¼ **cup sugar**
 2 **cups milk**
 2 **tsps. vanilla extract**

In a mixing bowl, whisk together the egg yolks and sugar for about 2 minutes. Set aside.

In a double boiler, over medium heat, bring milk and vanilla to a boil. Add the egg mixture to the milk and whisk quickly so eggs don't curdle. Cook until 145° is reached. Cool before serving.

RISSA ORIENTAL CAFE

THAI, JAPANESE, CHINESE CUISINE
1420 Main Street
St. Helena
963-7566
Monday–Saturday 11:30AM–9PM
AVERAGE DINNER FOR TWO: $22

AN ARRAY OF Thai, Japanese and Chinese delicacies in a comfortable setting—that's the hallmark of Rissa Oriental Cafe. Though scarcely two years old, Terra is touted by many as one of the finest restaurants in the Napa Valley.

The menu is distinctive, featuring fresh ingredients prepared in unusual combinations. Highlights include Gyoza (potstickers), Thai spicy beef salad and chicken coconut soup.

Great food in a friendly atmosphere at a modest price. That's hard to beat!

ORIENTAL CAFÉ

Chef Marta Avalle-Arce's Menu for Four

Chicken Coconut Soup
Gyoza
Thai Spicy Beef Salad

Chicken Coconut Soup

Serves 4
Preparation Time: 15 Minutes

 4 cups chicken stock
 3 cups coconut milk
 1 Tbsp. yellow curry paste
¼ cup fish sauce
 2 Tbsps. brown sugar
 2 Tbsps. soy sauce
 2 tomatoes cut into wedges
 1 lb. chicken meat, cut into small pieces
10–12 mushrooms, quartered
 1 small red onion, sliced thin
   Basil leaves
   Cilantro leaves
   Spinach leaves

Combine the chicken stock, coconut milk, curry paste, fish sauce, brown sugar and soy sauce to a boil, whisking well.

Add the tomato, chicken meat, mushrooms and onion. Simmer for 5 minutes or until chicken is almost done.

Add small sprinklings of basil, cilantro and spinach leaves. Serve immediately.

Gyoza (Potstickers)

Yield: 30
Preparation Time: 30 Minutes

    1 lb. ground pork
    2 cups cabbage, diced
    1 cup mushrooms, diced
    ¼ cup green onion stems, sliced
    ½ tsp. ground black pepper
    ½ tsp. sesame oil
    ½ tsp. fresh ginger, finely chopped
    ½ tsp. garlic, finely chopped
    1 Tbsp. soy sauce
    1 Tbsp. sweet cooking sake (Mirin)
      Potsticker wrappers
      Peanut oil

Bring pork to room temperature and knead until the fat binds to the pork. Add the cabbage, mushrooms, green onions, pepper, sesame oil, ginger, garlic, soy sauce and Mirin.

Place 1 Tbsp. of the mixture into the center of each potsticker wrapper. Moisten the edges lightly with water and fold the wrapper in half, pressing the edges together. Make sure the edge is tightly sealed.

Heat a small amount of peanut oil in a non-stick pan. Place as many potstickers in the pan as will fit comfortably, without crowding or overlapping. Sauté gently until the edges start to brown. Add enough water to half cover the potstickers. Cover the pan, turn heat to simmer and cook for 4 minutes or until the water has evaporated and the pork filling feels firm to the touch.

Turn the Goyza over, arrange on a platter and serve with Gyoza sauce.

Gyoza Sauce

Combine ½ cup rice wine vinegar, ½ cup soy sauce and 2 Tbsps. sesame chile oil. Garnish with toasted sesame seeds.

Thai Spicy Beef Salad

Serves 4
Preparation Time: 15 Minutes (note marinating time)

¼ cup soy sauce	¾ cup carrot, julienned
¼ cup brown sugar	1 small onion, sliced thin
¼ cup peanut oil	Mint leaves
2 Tbsps. green curry paste	Cilantro
2 tsps. curry powder	Basil leaves
1 Tbsp. fresh ginger	Cucumber slices for garnish
Juice of 1 lime	¾ cup roasted peanuts,
1 lb. beef tri-tip	chopped

Prepare marinade by combining the soy sauce, sugar, oil, curry paste and powder, ginger and lime.

Cut beef into thin strips and marinate for 2 hours. Grill or quickly pan-fry strips.

Mix with carrot, onion and small portions of mint, cilantro and basil leaves. Toss with enough dressing to coat meat and vegetables well. Top with cucumber slices and peanuts.

Dressing for Salad

2 Tbsps. fresh ginger, minced
1 Tbsp. jalapeño, minced
½ cup rice wine vinegar
2 Tbsps. soy sauce
2 Tbsps. brown sugar
2 Tbsps. chile oil (peanut oil heated with chile flakes)
2 Tbsps. fish sauce
Lettuce greens

Blend the ginger, jalapeño, vinegar, soy sauce, brown sugar, chile oil and fish sauce together. Toss lettuce with a small amount of dressing and mound in the center of individual plates.

SHOWLEY'S AT MIRAMONTE

CALIFORNIA CUISINE
1327 Railroad Avenue
St. Helena
963-1200
Lunch daily 11:30AM–3PM
Dinner daily 6PM–9PM
AVERAGE DINNER FOR TWO: $50

THE MAIN MIRAMONTE building was constructed in 1858, with smaller additions appended over the years. It has been operated as a restaurant almost continuously since 1880. Wood floors with a soft patina, asymmetrical walls, handmade window frames, heavy woodwork all marry into four gracious dining spaces. There is a brick floored patio sheltered by a century old fig tree. The interior design is more like a private home than a restaurant, with soft lighting, intimate spaces, an eclectic collection of art and a general feeling that your presence is truly desired here.

Comfortable as the restaurant is, dining well is the real reason for coming to Showley's. "West Coast Fresh" is the best description for the menu. Fresh ingredients prepared with care and attention are served by a gracious and welcoming staff.

SHOWLEY'S
AT MIRAMONTE

Chefs Grant & Sharon Showley's Menu for Six

Southwest Lasagne
Tuscan Bread
Roasted Chinese Game Hens
Fresh Berry Cobbler with Chantilly Cream

Southwest Lasagne Sauce

Preparation Time: 10 Minutes

1 **medium onion, finely chopped**
2 **Tbsps. butter**
1 **Tbsp. garlic, finely chopped**
2 **Tbsps. chile powder**
1 **tsp. cumin, ground**
2 **Tbsps. flour**
1 **cup chicken stock**
½ **cup water**
   Salt and white pepper

Sauté the onion in butter until lightly golden. Add garlic, chile powder and cumin, cooking for 1 minute.

Add flour and whisk until incorporated. Add stock and continue to cook until thickened. Add water if necessary. Season with salt and pepper.

Serve the sauce with the lasagne.

Southwest Lasagne

Serves 6
Preparation Time: 1 Hour
Pre-heat oven to 350°

½ **cup cream**
 2 **eggs**
 1 **log Montrachet goat cheese, approx. 6 oz.**
½ **cup ricotta cheese**
10 **large tortillas**
 2 **jars whole pimentos**
½ **cup pesto**
½ **cup pine nuts, lightly roasted**
 1 **large can whole chiles**
 3 **cups grated cheddar cheese**

In a mixer, blend the cream, eggs, goat cheese and ricotta cheese. Set aside.

Butter one lasagne pan. Set aside.

Lightly grill the 10 tortillas.

Layer 1: Place two tortillas into the lasagne pan. Top with the red pimientos.

Layer 2: Top with two more tortillas and spread the cheese mixture.

Layer 3: Follow with two more tortillas and top with pesto and pine nuts.

Layer 4: Follow with two more tortillas and top with the chiles and cheddar cheese.

Layer 5: Top lasagne with 2 tortillas.

Cover with foil and bake 45 minutes at 350.°

Tuscan Bread

Serves 6
Preparation Time: 3 Hours

2 cups warm water
1 package yeast
2 Tbsps. salt
½ cup walnuts, chopped
2 lbs. flour, preferably hard wheat (bakers' flour)

Mix together water and yeast until dissolved. Add salt and walnuts and slowly add flour. Knead until smooth, but no longer sticking
to the palm of your hand.

Place into a buttered bowl, cover with plastic wrap. Let rise to
double in bulk, approximately 2 hours.

Pre-heat oven to 350.° Remove dough from bowl onto floured cut-
ting board. Cut into two pieces and form into two long loaves. Place
onto cookie sheet dusted with flour and place into oven.

Bake for 1 hour or until the bottom of the loaf sounds hollow
when tapped.

Chinese Game Hens

Serves 6
Preparation Time: 1 Hour (note marinating time)

  6 Cornish game hens
  ¼ cup light soy sauce
  ¼ cup heavy soy sauce
  ¼ cup hoisin sauce
  2 Tbsps. sesame oil
  1 bunch green onions, chopped
  1 small piece ginger, peeled, chopped
  1 Tbsp. garlic, chopped
  1 Tbsp. chile paste
  1 tsp. sugar
  1 Tbsp. sherry
  Cilantro sprigs for garnish

Cut along the back of each game hen to butterfly and spread apart. Set aside.

Prepare the marinade by mixing together the soy sauces, hoisin, sesame oil, onion, ginger, garlic, chile paste, sugar and sherry. Marinate hens for several hours.

Pre-heat oven to 400.° Remove hens from marinade and place on a foil-lined cookie sheet. Roast for 40 minutes, brushing with reserved marinade every 20 minutes.

Game hen is done when juices run clean when pierced with the tip of a knife.

Garnish with cilantro sprigs.

Berry Cobbler with Chantilly Cream

Serves 6
Preparation Time: 45 Minutes
Pre-heat oven to 350°

 ¾ lb. fresh or frozen berries
 ¾ cup walnuts, chopped
 2 cups sugar
 3 eggs, beaten
1¼ cups flour
 ¾ cup butter, melted

Grease a 9 × 12″ pan. Place berries on bottom of pan.

In a mixing bowl, combine the walnuts and 1 cup sugar. Cover berries with walnut mixture.

In a separate bowl, combine the remaining sugar, beaten eggs and flour. Stir in melted butter. Cover berries with egg mixture.

Bake 40 minutes or until golden brown. Serve with powdered sugar and chantilly cream.

Chantilly Cream

1 cup whipping cream
½ cup powdered sugar
1 tsp. vanilla extract

Beat whipping cream. Add sugar and vanilla.

STARMONT AT MEADOWOOD

CALIFORNIA NOUVELLE CUISINE
900 Meadowood Lane
St. Helena
963-3646, 800-458-8080
Dinner daily 5:30PM–10PM
Sunday brunch 11:AM–2PM
AVERAGE DINNER FOR TWO: $65

FOR A QUARTER of a century, Meadowood has been an exclusive private club enjoyed by the local gentry. Now, discriminating travellers can discover this magical resort hotel. What once was only a private reserve is now open to the public.

Sequestered on 250 wooded acres, Meadowood offers warm hospitality, privacy and service along with all the facilities that enhance creativity and rejuvenate your sense of well being. Throughout the year Meadowood's Wine School offers unique wine and food courses for experts and neophytes alike, and every June there is a crescendo of excitement when Meadowood hosts the prestigious Napa Valley Wine Auction.

Overlooking the tree-lined golf course, the very romantic Starmont Restaurant is comfortably luxurious. The cuisine reflects an understanding of continental traditions and sparkles with country innovations.

Chef Henri Delcros' Menu for Four

Roast Duck with Honey
Shrimp in Cabbage Leaves with Basil Sauce
Fresh Berries with Champagne Sabayon

Roast Duck with Honey

Serves 4
Preparation Time: 45 Minutes
Pre-heat oven to 400°

 4 breasts of Muscovy ducks
 ½ cup honey
 4 Tbsps. red wine vinegar
 1 qt. red wine
 2 Tbsps. butter, melted
 2 Tbsps. flour

Roast duck breasts until golden brown, approximately 10 minutes at 400.°

In a 2 qt. pan, caramelize honey over medium heat, until thick and golden brown. Add red wine vinegar and caramelize again. Add red wine and simmer until reduced by half, approximately 15 minutes.

Make a roux by combining the butter and flour over low heat. Strain through a mesh sieve and add to the honey mixture to thicken.

Arrange duck on a serving platter and pour sauce over duck before serving.

Shrimp in Cabbage Leaves with Basil Sauce

Serves 4
Preparation Time: 15 Minutes

16 shrimp
 1 head savoy cabbage
    Basil sauce

Peel and devein shrimp and steam for 2–3 minutes. Set aside.

Clean and wash cabbage leaves. Cook rapidly in boiling water until cabbage is al dente. Remove leaves promptly and rinse under cold water. Drain on towel.

Place 1 or 2 shrimp in center of cabbage leaf, folding the leaf over to secure. Place in steamer and reheat for 2 minutes over boiling water.

Serve with warm basil sauce drizzled over the wrapped shrimp.

Basil Sauce

¾ **cup shallots, finely chopped**
 4 large garlic cloves, crushed
 1 bunch fresh basil, finely chopped
⅓ **cup fresh tarragon, chopped**
⅓ **cup chervil, chopped**
 1 cup olive oil
    Salt and pepper to taste

Mix the first 5 ingredients together. Add olive oil and combine. Season to taste with salt and pepper.

Serve over shrimp in cabbage leaves.

Fresh Berries
with Champagne Sabayon

Serves 4
Preparation Time: 20 Minutes

  4 egg yolks
  ½ cup cream
  2 Tbsps. sugar
  1 cup champagne brut
  Fresh strawberries

Combine the egg yolks, cream, sugar and champagne into a stainless steel saucepan. Over a low flame, mix constantly until the mixture becomes thick.

Remove from heat and pour the sabayon over fresh berries.

Serve immediately.

Terra Restaurant

SOUTHERN FRENCH, NORTHERN ITALIAN CUISINE
1345 Railroad Ave.
St. Helena
963-8931
Monday, Wednesday, Thursday, Sunday 6PM–9:30PM
Friday–Saturday 6PM–10PM
AVERAGE DINNER FOR TWO: $60

MODESTLY, GINGERLY, yet another culinary giant has slipped into the Napa Valley. What began quietly in November '88 when Hiro Sone, Wolfgang Puck's former head chef at Spago, and his wife Lissa Doumani, a Spago pastry chef, opened Terra Restaurant in St. Helena's historic Hatchery Building, has turned quickly into a profound statement of culinary excellence. Terra now joins the ever-growing number of widely acclaimed restaurants to take up residence in America's premier wine-growing region.

The result is masterful presentations of such earthy delicacies as entrees of Osso Bucco with Risotto Milanese, Grilled Rack of Lamb with Tuscan White Beans, and Seared Pepper Salmon with Tomato Mint Vinaigrette. Delightful appetizers of Baked Mussels in Garlic Butter and Smoked Bacon and Wild Mushrooms in Puff Pastry grace the appetizer portion of the menu. A most unusual Tiramisu headlines a sumptuous array of desserts.

There is a oneness at Terra created by the simplistic attraction of the food, the stately warmth of the stone restaurant structure and the friendly environment created by the guests who dine here.

Warm Scallop Salad with Lemon Coriander Vinaigrette

1¼ lbs. scallops, ¼″ thick
1 cup extra virgin olive oil
½ cup lemon juice
½ cup tomatoes, finely chopped
1 Tbsp. coriander seeds, roasted
 Salt and pepper to taste
2 Tbsps. chives, chopped

Place scallops on a serving plate in the broiler until warm, not fully cooked. Remove from heat.

Meanwhile, prepare the vinaigrette by combining the olive oil, lemon juice, tomatoes, and coriander seeds over low heat. Salt and pepper to taste.

Pour the warm vinaigrette over the scallops and return to the broiler until the scallops are cooked.

Sprinkle with chives and serve hot.

Medallions of Lamb
with Black Olive Anchovy Sauce

Serves 6
Preparation Time: 45 Minutes (note marinating time)

6 lamb loins, ½ lb. each
2 Tbsps. olive oil
2 tsps. thyme, chopped
1 tsp. rosemary, chopped
1 tsp. garlic, chopped
1 Tbsp. butter
½ cup white wine
1 cup lamb stock
¼ cup tomato purée
2 Tbsps. tapenade
Salt and pepper to taste

Rub the lamb loins with olive oil. Season with 1 tsp. thyme and rosemary. Allow to marinate for a least one hour prior to grilling.

Prepare the sauce by sautéing the garlic in butter until lightly brown. Add the white wine and reduce to 1 Tbsp. Add lamb stock and tomato purée and reduce to 1 cup. Add tapenade, salt and pepper. Set aside.

Grill the lamb loins.

To serve, place warm sauce on plates with sliced lamb on top.

Strawberry Shortcake with Crème Fraîche

Serves 6
Preparation Time: 45 Minutes (note refrigeration time)

1½ **cups flour**
½ **tsp. baking powder**
¼ **tsp. salt**
½ **cup sugar**
6 **Tbsps. butter, thinly sliced**
1½ **cups cream**
1 **tsp. vanilla extract**
2 **cups crème fraîche**
3 **cups raspberry**
1 **tsp. lemon juice**
3 **cups strawberries, chopped**
1 **cup blueberries, chopped**
1 **cup blackberries, chopped**
½ **cup powdered sugar**

Prepare the shortcake dough by combining in a mixer the flour, baking powder, salt, 3 Tbsps. sugar and butter until crumbly. Add ½ cup cream and ½ tsp. vanilla extract.

Remove from mixer and roll out dough. Cut dough with a biscuit cutter, place on baking sheet and chill for 1 hour.

Bake at 350° for 15 minutes. Remove from oven and cool.

Mix together the crème fraîche, 1 cup cream, ⅓ cup sugar and ½ tsp. vanilla extract. Set aside.

Prepare the berry purée by combining 2 cups raspberry, lemon juice and 3 Tbsps. sugar in a blender. Purée and strain. Set aside.

Prepare the berry mixture by combining the strawberries, blueberries, 1 cup of raspberries, blackberries and powdered sugar together in a mixing bowl. Refrigerate.

To serve, cut shortcake in half. Place bottom half on plate and top with crème fraîche. Layer berry mixture on top and drizzle with the berry purée over the shortcake. Place the top half of the shortcake on top.

TRA VIGNE

ITALIAN CUISINE
1050 Charter Oak
St. Helena
963-4444
Open daily 12 Noon–10PM
AVERAGE DINNER FOR TWO: $60

To DESCRIBE TRA VIGNE as "just a restaurant" would overlook portions of its true character. "Italian villa" more fairly fits the property. "Italian inspired" is the preferred term.

In the spring and summer, the courtyard is awash with color, fragrances and greenery. However, it is the restaurant's interior that gives one the feel of refined elegance. Thirty-foot ceilings, an original hand-carved bar and majestic Italian beaded light fixtures all help create an elegant and sophisticated atmosphere.

Chef Michael Chiarello says of his menu, "California food products prepared with the eyes, hand and heart of an Italian." The collaboration of Italian and American innovation can be found every day at Tra Vigne. Antipasti are particularly intriguing. Pastas are equally superb, embracing both American and Italian interpretations that one might not expect to see in the same dish.

The food, as well as the surroundings, have made Tra Vigne a unique complement to the Napa Valley.

Chef Michael Chiarello's Menu for Four

Grilled Mozzarella with Sun-dried Tomato Vinaigrette
Seafood Soup (Brodetto)
Harvest Foccacia Bread
Fettucine with Grilled Artichokes

Grilled Mozzarella

Serves 4
Preparation Time: 15 Minutes

4 large romaine leaves
1 lb. fresh mozzarella, cut into 4 squares
Salt and pepper
⅛ lb. prosciutto, diced
Olive oil

Blanch the romaine leaves in boiling salted water for 30 seconds. Remove and immediately immerse in ice water to stop the cooking process. Drain, then pat the leaves dry.

Lay out the leaves, rib side down. Place a square of cheese in the middle of each leaf. Sprinkle with salt and pepper, then top each piece of cheese with ¼ of the diced prosciutto. Fold in the edges of the leaves like an envelope (or diaper). Brush with oil.

Grill over a medium to hot flame until the cheese begins to weep. Transfer to a plate of seasonal mixed greens that have been dressed with the sun-dried tomato vinaigrette. (Recipe follows).

Sun-dried Tomato Vinaigrette

Serves 4
Preparation Time: 10 Minutes (note refrigeration time)

½ **cup sun-dried tomatoes, minced**
1 **tsp. garlic, minced**
12 **fresh basil leaves**
½ **cup extra virgin olive oil**
¼ **cup balsamic vinegar**
 Black pepper to taste

Combine all ingredients in a non-reactive bowl. Mix well and let stand at least 1 hour before serving.

Cooking tip: If you are using sun-dried tomatoes packed in oil you can mince them as they are. If you are using dry sun-dried tomatoes you must rehydrate them before use.

Seafood Soup (Brodetto)

Serves 4
Preparation Time: 45 Minutes

1 live dungeness crab, 2–3 lbs.
3 cups white wine
Juice of 2 lemons
4 bay leaves
2 Tbsps. pickling spice
¼ cup salt
1 lb. prawns, peeled, deveined,
  reserve shells
Olive oil
4 tsps. garlic, chopped
4 Tbsps. Pernod
4 cups tomato, peeled,
  seeded, diced
Pinch of saffron
4 cups fish stock
2 lbs. clams
2 lbs. mussels
½ tsp. chile flakes
1 Tbsp. butter
1 sprig each basil, Italian
  parsley, tarragon, chopped

Prepare the crab by blanching in solution of 1½ gallons water to 2 cups white wine, lemon juice, bay leaves, pickling spice and salt. Bring liquid to a rapid boil. Add crab, and when water returns to a boil, simmer for 6–8 minutes. Remove and cool. When cooled, clean and crack legs and body to remove crab meat.

Prepare the stock by toasting shrimp shells in hot olive oil until golden brown. Add 1 Tbsp. garlic and caramelize. Deglaze with 2 Tbsps. Pernod. Add 2 cups chopped tomatoes and 1 cup white wine. Add saffron and simmer for 5 minutes. Add fish stock and cook until reduced by half. Strain and reserve.

To assemble brodetto, heat 4 Tbsps. olive oil in a large skillet or sauté pan. Add clams and mussels. When shells open, add shrimp and sauté to golden brown. Remove seafood and set aside with pre-pared crab.

To the same pan, add 1 tsp. garlic and chile flakes. When garlic is golden brown, deglaze the pan with remaining Pernod. Add remaining tomatoes and the brodetto stock. Simmer until sauce begins to thicken slightly. Add reserved seafood, butter and fresh herbs.

Harvest Foccacia

Serves 4
Preparation Time: 1½ Hours

  1 small cake fresh yeast or 2½ tsps. dry
 ½ cup warm milk
  1 Tbsp. sugar
  8 cups all-purpose flour
  1 cup fresh grapes
  1 cup golden raisins
  2 Tbsps. fresh rosemary
1⅛ cups virgin olive oil
  2 cups warm water
  1 Tbsp. coarse salt

Mix the yeast, milk, sugar and ½ cup flour in mixing bowl. Let stand to foam for 15 minutes

Prepare the filling by warming 1 cup olive oil on medium heat. Add the grapes, raisins and rosemary. When warm, remove from heat and let set until room temperature.

Mix half of the filling into the yeast mixture. Add 4 cups flour and mix, using dough attachment on mixer. Mix until smooth, adding salt and remaining flour one cup at a time. Knead in machine for 3 minutes. Dough should be velvety and elastic. Set in an oiled bowl with damp cloth on top to rise, approximately 1 hour.

Coat a cookie pan with olive oil. Roll out dough to fit inside the pan. Cover with damp cloth and rise a second time, until doubled in volume. Press finger indents into dough, making sure not to puncture all the way through. Spread remaining topping on top of dough. Sprinkle with 1 Tbsp. each sugar and salt on top and bake in 350° oven until golden brown.

Cooking note: This bread is typically made in Italy with the raisins from a previously successful harvest and the grapes from the current harvest as a good luck snack to be eaten during crush.

Fettucine with Grilled Artichokes

Serves 4
Preparation Time: 20 Minutes

- 4 **fresh artichoke hearts**
  Juice of 1 lemon
- 4 **Tbsps. olive oil**
- 1 **head garlic, peeled, cloves crushed**
- 4 **cups chicken stock**
- ½ **cup corn**
- 2 **Tbsps. chervil, chopped**
- 2 **tsps. marjoram, chopped**
- 3 **Tbsps. butter**
  Salt and pepper to taste
  Fresh fettucine

Prepare artichoke hearts by rubbing with lemon juice and 2 Tbsps. olive oil. Grill until tender. Slice thin.

In a large sauté pan, heat 2 Tbsps. olive oil to the smoking point, then reduce heat to medium. Add garlic and sauté until golden brown. Add sliced artichokes and toss well. Add chicken stock and reduce until sauce begins to take on body. Add corn, chervil, marjoram and butter. Simmer until butter has been incorporated, then adjust seasonings with salt and pepper as needed.

Cook fresh pasta in rapidly boiling salted water until firm to the tooth or al dente. Drain and toss with the sauce.

Serve immediately.

TRILOGY

FRENCH CUISINE
1234 Main Street
St. Helena
963-5507
Lunch Tuesday–Friday 12 Noon–2PM
Dinner Tuesday–Saturday 6PM–9PM
AVERAGE DINNER FOR TWO: $32

WITHOUT A DOUBT, Trilogy is one of the locals' most popular restaurants—and with good reason.

Specializing in French cuisine with a California emphasis, Trilogy lightens the classics and offers both simple and complex dishes.

Menu highlights include Grilled Sea Scallops with Black Olive and Tomato Vinaigrette, Roasted Rack of Lamb with Whole Grain Mustard Sauce and Sautéed Medallions of Veal with Shiitake Mushrooms and Sherry.

Trilogy offers a warm, friendly atmosphere, an extensive wine list and exceptional service.

Chef Diane Pariseau's Menu for Four

Steamed Halibut with Lemon Grass and Ginger
Polenta with Red Bell Pepper Sauce
White Chocolate Mousse Torte

Steamed Halibut with Lemon Grass and Ginger

Serves 4
Preparation Time: 15 Minutes

  1 **stalk of lemon grass**
  1 **1-inch piece of ginger root, peeled**
  3 **garlic cloves, peeled**
  ⅛ **tsp. cayenne pepper (optional)**
  3 **tsps. sesame oil**
  1½ **Tbsps. rice wine vinegar**
  1 **tsp. salt**
  4 **Halibut filets**

In a food processor or using a mortar and pestle, grind the lemon grass, ginger and garlic, until paste looks slightly fibrous. Add remaining ingredients.

Spread paste on fish and steam in water until done, approximately 5–7 minutes.

Cooking tip: This recipe lends itself well to monkfish or salmon.

Polenta with Red Bell Pepper Sauce

Serves 4
Preparation Time: 25 Minutes (note refrigeration time)

3 cups water or chicken stock
   Salt and pepper to taste
1 clove garlic, chopped
1 cup polenta
1 tsp. thyme
1 tsp. oregano
   Olive oil

Bring water or stock to a boil with salt, pepper and garlic. In a slow, steady steam, add polenta to the mixture and continue to stir until very thick. Add the herbs to the mixture and stir for 1 minute.

Pour into a 9″ greased pie plate and chill well. Cut into desired size and brush with olive oil before grilling.

Red Bell Pepper Sauce

Preparation Time: 15 Minutes

2 red bell peppers, roasted, peeled
1 clove garlic
1 cup olive oil
   Salt and pepper to taste

Purée garlic in a blender with the peppers. While the blender is still running, add the olive oil in a slow stream. When smooth, season with salt and pepper to taste.

Serve at room temperature over the polenta.

White Chocolate Mousse Torte

Serves 4
Preparation Time: 30 Minutes (note refrigeration time)

¾ **lb. white chocolate**
8 **Tbsps. butter**
⅔ **cup milk**
1 **Tbsps. gelatin**
4 **egg whites**
2 **cups heavy cream, whipped**

Melt the chocolate and butter over a double boiler.

In a mixing bowl, dissolve gelatin in cold milk. Add the gelatin to the chocolate mix and cool to room temperature.

Whip room-temperature egg whites and fold into the cooled chocolate mixture. Fold in the whipped cream and pour into a 10″ springform pan with crust. (Recipe follows).

Crust

Preparation Time: 10 Minutes

½ **cup sugar**
½ **cup almonds**
½ **cup butter**
1 **cup flour**

In a food processor, grind sugar and almonds. Set aside.

Melt butter in sauté pan and add the flour. Cook over low heat for 3–4 minutes. Add the almond mix and cook for another 3–4 minutes.

Press crust mixture flat into a 10″ springform pan. Pour in chocolate mixture and refrigerate until firm.

Sonoma County:
The Valley of the Moon

It WAS WRITER Jack London who translated the original name of Sonoma County. The Indians called it Tso-noma: The Valley of the Moon.

One of the state's 27 original counties, Sonoma was first spotted by Europeans in 1775, when Spanish explorer Juan Francisco de Bodega sailed into what is now Bodega Bay.

But it wasn't just the Spanish who had their eyes on Sonoma County. The Russians also liked what they saw. However, it took the lowly gopher to upset the Russians' plans.

At the start of the 19th century, Russia was pushing eastward into Alaska, encouraged by the lucrative sea otter fur business. Furs, food and supplies were running short at Sitka, Alaska, so the Russians set out for San Francisco to buy food. Along the way, they noticed promising (and undefended) land north of San Francisco.

In 1812, 700 Russians settled at a rocky inlet north of Bodega Bay. Calling it Ross, an old term for Russia, they built a wooden fort and set upon the defenseless sea otters.

Their HUNTING METHOD was simple: they captured a sea otter pup and held it—screaming—until its parents surfaced to be killed. In one year, 200,000 otter pelts were sent back to Russia. Business was good and the Russians settled in.

They planted crops and developed Fort Ross. But eventually they wiped out the otter population and the Russians had to depend more and more on their crops.

But the gophers (the Russians called them underground rats) were hungry too. They quickly devoured all the crops.

*Mexican General
Mariano Vallejo,
at age 60.
He founded Sonoma
in 1835.*

BANKRUPTCY AND HUNGER stared the Russians in the face. In 1840, they sold the fort to John A. Sutter of Sacramento.

The fort, still displaying the six-sided church steeple and crooked doubled cross, is now a state park in the process of being restored. It's well worth a stop.

While the Russians were encamped at Fort Ross, 50 miles southeast in Sonoma, the last of the California Missions—Mission San Francisco Solano—was established in 1823. By 1835, Mexican General Mariano Vallejo founded the pueblo of Sonoma.

But more and more American settlers arrived every day. And, in 1846—three years before the start of the Gold Rush—the Bear Flag Revolt took place in Sonoma. A small group of American settlers, encouraged by General John C. Fremont, captured General Vallejo and proclaimed California a republic.

SEVERAL INCIDENTS from these days are worth retelling.

One involved a brutal form of entertainment: pitting bulls and grizzly bears against one another in fights to the death. Behind the soldiers' barracks in Sonoma, a corral and viewing stands were erected. The price of admission was 25 cents.

There was one handicap: the bears had their hind legs bound, so the bulls usually won.

ANOTHER SONOMA INCIDENT added a notorious word to the English language. "Fighting Joe" Hooker, a West Point graduate, was appointed adjutant of the Pacific Division and was stationed at Sonoma in 1849.

By 1851, he was forced to resign because of charges of profiteering and conduct unbecoming an officer. He was accused of buying goods and selling them at exorbitant rates to the Army.

Joe Hooker tried his hand at farming, but that didn't work out well. Mostly he hung around town, playing cards and chasing women.

One day, the story goes, two new recruits who were assigned to the Sonoma post asked if there were any loose women around.

The older soldiers told them there were no loose women. But the recruits noticed two likely-looking girls sashaying around the post.

"How about those?" the recruits asked.

The reply was: "They're Hooker's."

Hooker did end up with a Civil War command in charge of the Army of the Potomac in the Battle of Chancellorsville.

But he will always be remembered best for the name he lent to loose women.

THE FERTILE Sonoma, Santa Rosa and Russian River valleys added much to the quality of life of California. Bountiful crops included apples, prunes and, of course, wine grapes.

In addition, water was plentiful, as were venison, bear, fish and fowl, gambling houses and restaurants.

Many Italians came to the area directly from Italy to work in the local quarries, producing cobblestones for the streets of San Francisco.

They also brought a knowledge of viticulture and introduced a resistant root to replace the diseased grape vines of Sonoma County.

The Miller and Pauli store still stands in Sonoma, now housing a gift shop. The man in the white coat leaning against the hitching rail at left is Salvador Vallejo, brother of General Vallejo.

THE ITALIANS also brought their love of fine food to go along with fine wines.

The stage was set for a melding of cultural tastes.

The spices and cuisines of Swiss, Italians, Mexicans, Chinese, French, Spanish and all the cultures of the settlers took fruit in Sonoma County.

The wines improved year by year.

And today we reap the bounty: the heavenly tastes of the Valley of the Moon.

BLUE HERON

CALIFORNIA CUISINE
Hwy. 116 & Moscow Road
Duncans Mills
865-2225
Summer: open 7 days a week
Dining room 5PM–9:30PM
Bar opens 4PM, Sunday Brunch 10AM–2PM
Winter: call for days and times
AVERAGE DINNER FOR TWO: $35

THE "BLUE," AS the locals call this restaurant, began with an innovative, high-quality vegetarian menu in 1977. Today however, homemade soups, pastas, assorted fresh salads, meats, fresh fish and poultry, not to mention wonderful desserts, are featured.

The redwood interior of the dining room is enhanced with garden-grown fresh flowers. Garden flowers enter the kitchen as well. Each plate is garnished with edible flowers and herbs such as violas, nasturtium, lavender and rose.

The Blue Heron's atmosphere is casual, featuring live classical guitar, yet is special enough for the most important dinner occasion.

Chef Scott Reed's Menu for Four

Baked Brie with Pesto
Lemon Herb Vinaigrette
Broiled Swordfish with Wasabi Butter
Kahlua Chocolate Mousse

Baked Brie with Pesto

Serves 4
Preparation Time: 15 Minutes
Pre-heat oven to 400°

½ **lb. Brie**
 2 **tsps. pesto sauce, recipe follows**
 2 **cloves garlic, pressed**
   Loaf of sourdough bread

Place pesto in the bottom of small Pyrex or oven-proof casserole or custard dish. Press garlic into dish. Place Brie on top of pesto and bake until cheese is soft and gently bubbling.

Serve immediately with warmed sourdough bread.

Cooking tip: Marinated artichoke hearts and Greek olives accompany this appetizer well.

Pesto Sauce

Preparation Time: 20 Minutes
Yields 2 cups

  2 **cups fresh basil leaves**
  4 **garlic cloves, pressed**
  1 **cup pine nuts or walnuts**
  1 **cup olive oil**
  1 **cup fresh Parmesan cheese, grated**
 ¼ **cup fresh Romano cheese, grated**
     Salt and pepper to taste

In a food processor, combine the basil, garlic and nuts. When the mixture is well blended, slowly add the olive oil, while the processor is running. Add cheeses, salt and pepper and process until blended.
Cover and refrigerate.

Lemon Herb Vinaigrette

Preparation Time: 15 Minutes
Yields 5 cups dressing

2 ¼ cups corn oil
1 cup olive oil
¾ cup lemon juice
½ cup red wine vinegar
¼ cup honey
1 ½ Tbsps. salt
4 large garlic cloves, pressed
1 ½ tsps. Dijon mustard
1 ½ tsps. curry powder
2 ¼ tsps. ground cumin
2 ¼ tsps. basil
1 tsp. paprika
1 tsp. oregano
1 tsp. dill
1 tsp. tarragon
1 tsp. chervil

In a large mixing bowl, combine both oils, lemon juice, vinegar and honey.

Add the salt, garlic, mustard, curry powder and cumin.

Whisk in the dried herbs and refrigerate.

Cooking tip: The dressing tastes best made one day prior to serving. This vinaigrette will keep for months in the refrigerator.

Broiled Swordfish Steaks with Wasabi Butter

Serves 4
Preparation Time: 20 Minutes

2 lbs. swordfish, cut into 8 oz. steaks
1 cube butter, melted
3 cloves garlic, pressed
  Salt and pepper to taste
  Dry vermouth to taste

Pre-heat broiler. Brush melted butter on shallow broiling pan. Add garlic, salt and pepper. Place swordfish steaks in pan and brush fish with remaining butter. Add enough dry Vermouth to assure that there will be a basting fluid.

Broil 6 inches from heat. Baste often. No need to turn steaks over. Cook until done.

Top each steak with Wasabi Butter.

Wasabi Butter

Preparation Time: 20 Minutes

2 Tbsps. Wasabi (powdered Japanese horseradish)
1 cube salted butter, room temperature
3 pinches salt

Place wasabi powder in a glass bowl, adding enough cold water to form a paste. Set aside for 10 minutes.

Cream butter with electric beater. Add horseradish paste, salt and beat well.

Cover and refrigerate.

Cooking tip: Wasabi Butter is great on steamed vegetables, sushi, steak and grilled prawns.

Kahlua Chocolate Mousse

Preparation Time: 30 Minutes (note refrigeration time)

      3 large eggs, separated
   ½ lb. dark bittersweet chocolate
      6 Tbsps. Kahlua
      1 tsp. brown sugar
   1½ cups whipping cream
      1 tsp. vanilla extract

Separate egg yolks and whites into separate bowls, keeping eggs at room temperature. Beat yolks until blended, beat egg whites until stiff.

Melt chocolate in double boiler. Set aside.

Place Kahlua and brown sugar in small sauce pan on medium heat until the sugar dissolves. Don't boil. Set aside.

Blend the egg yolks into the warm chocolate. Add the Kahlua mixture and blend until the chocolate mixture is shiny and smooth. Remove from heat.

While chocolate is cooling, whip the cream and vanilla together until stiff.

When chocolate has cooled, gently fold in the egg whites. Add the cream and blend well.

Spoon into dessert glasses and chill for 2 hours. Serve topped with toasted almonds.

Cooking tip: Use a wooden spoon to beat the egg yolks and Kahlua into chocolate.

CAFFE PORTOFINO RISTORANTE & BAR

ITALIAN CUISINE
535 4th Street
Santa Rosa
523-1171
Lunch Monday–Saturday 11:30AM–5PM
Dinner Monday–Thursday 5PM–10PM
Friday & Saturday 5PM–11PM
AVERAGE DINNER FOR TWO: $35

THE WORDS AUTHENTIC and traditional may best describe the outstanding European cuisine and pleasant atmosphere within the rustic brick walls of Caffe Portofino. The award-winning ristorante has become well known and highly regarded for its detailed attention to flavor and authenticity, as well as its dedication to an extensive California and European wine list.

A house speciality is the homemade ravioli, which is stuffed with chicken, salmon, duck, artichoke hearts or even rabbit.

Located in downtown Santa Rosa, Caffe Portofino is a favored Sonoma County meeting place for locals as well as visitors.

CAFFÈ
Portofino
Ristorante & Bar

Pork with Bay Leaves
Agnolotti Pasta with Cream
Amaretti-Stuffed Peaches

Pork with Bay Leaves

Serves 6
Preparation Time: 2 Hours

 2 Tbsps. extra virgin olive oil
 1 loin of pork, about 2 lbs.
 1 Tbsp. juniper berries, finely chopped
 2 whole cloves
10 bay leaves
 2 medium onions, chopped
   Salt and freshly ground pepper
 1 cup dry white wine

Heat the oil in a saucepan just large enough to hold the meat. Add pork and brown it over moderate heat for about 10 minutes. Add juniper berries, cloves, bay leaves, onions, salt and pepper.

Lower the heat and cook the meat until very tender, about 1½ hours, adding ½ cup wine a little at a time.

Slice the meat and arrange on a serving dish. Pour the remaining wine into the pan and bring to a boil, scraping up browned bits. Put this sauce through a sieve and pour over the meat.

Serve immediately.

Agnolotti Pasta with Cream

Serves 6
Preparation Time: 45 Minutes

1¼ cups young beet greens or spinach leaves
⅓ cup ricotta
⅓ cup chicken, finely chopped
⅓ cup cooked ham, finely chopped
1 cup Parmesan cheese, grated
4 eggs
  Pinch of nutmeg
  Salt and freshly ground pepper
2½ cups all-purpose flour
3 Tbsps. butter
1 cup cream

Cook the beet greens or spinach leaves in boiling, salted water, until just wilted. Squeeze dry and chop very finely.

In a large mixing bowl, prepare the filling by combining the ricotta, chicken, ham, ¼ cup Parmesan cheese, 1 egg, nutmeg, pepper and the cooked spinach.

Prepare the pasta dough by combining the flour and 3 eggs. Knead until smooth and elastic. Roll out very thinly. Place small balls of the filling at 2½" intervals over half the sheet of dough. Fold the dough over to cover filling, pressing with the fingers around each ball. Using a pastry wheel with fluted edge, cut out agnolotti in half-moon or square shapes.

Bring a large pot of water to boil over high heat. Drop in agnolotti and cook until al dente.

While the pasta is cooking, heat the butter and cream over low heat. Arrange agnolotti in a serving dish and pour butter and cream over the pasta. Sprinkle with ¾ cup Parmesan cheese and serve.

Amaretti-Stuffed Peaches

Serves 6
Preparation Time: 20 Minutes

½ **cup white wine**
½ **cup sugar**
 6 **ripe peaches, peeled, halved, pitted**
12 **Amaretti biscuits, crushed**
 1 **egg yolk, beaten**
 3 **Tbsps. cream, whipped**

Boil the wine and sugar for 5 minutes to form a syrup. Poach the peach halves in the syrup for 5 minutes, then lift the peaches out with a slotted spoon. Let cool.

Fold the Amaretti crumbs and egg yolk into the whipped cream. Fill the peach halves with this cream mixture.

Arrange on a serving plate and pour the remaining wine syrup around them.

Serve immediately.

CHATEAU SOUVERAIN

AMERICAN FRENCH CUISINE
400 Souverain Road
Geyserville
433-3141
Lunch Tuesday–Saturday 11:30AM–3PM
Dinner Thursday–Saturday 5:30PM–9PM
Sunday Brunch 10AM–2:30PM
AVERAGE DINNER FOR TWO: $75

HIGH ATOP A vine-covered knoll overlooking the un-spoiled beauty of the Alexander Valley is Chateau Souverain—one of the viticultural and architectural landmarks of Northern California's wine-producing region. At Chateau Souverain, visitors to Sonoma County can enjoy a four-star restaurant right at the winery.

Both on the outdoor terrace and in the beam-ceilinged dining room, the views are spectacular. The atmosphere is relaxed, yet elegant.

Each day the restaurant offers an intriguing selection of dishes based on the freshest and finest local produce, many prepared in the classic French Country manner.

The wine list features all the wines of Chateau Souverain, plus a wide selection of other fine Sonoma County wines.

CHATEAU
SOUVERAIN®

94

Chef Patricia Windisch's Menu for Six

*Cream of Arugula Soup
with Oysters & Garlic Butter
Squab on Sage Pasta
Raspberry Amaretto Custard Tarts*

Garlic Butter

*Serves 6
Preparation Time: 10 Minutes*

1 **cup butter, unsalted**
2 **Tbsps. parsley, chopped**
2 **tsps. Worchestershire sauce**
1 **tsp. Tabasco**
2 **tsps. lemon juice**
1 **tsp. shallots, chopped**
6 **cloves garlic, chopped fine**
  Salt and pepper to taste

Soften butter and mix in the remaining ingredients. Serve in the cream of arugula soup. (Recipe follows).

Cooking tip: This garlic butter is usually served with escargots.

Cream of Arugula Soup

Serves 6
Preparation Time: 30 Minutes

   ¼ **lb. arugula**
   6 **shallots, diced fine**
   4 **Tbsps. butter**
   2 **qts. chicken stock**
  24 **oysters, shucked, reserve juices**
   2 **Tbsps. cornstarch**
  2¼ **cups cream**
      Juice of ½ lemon
   ½ **cup crème fraîche or sour cream**
      Salt and pepper to taste
      Arugula flowers for garnish

Clean the arugula and remove stems. Blanch in hot water for 30 seconds. Set aside.

Sauté shallots in butter until transparent. Add the blanched arugula, chicken stock and oyster juices. Bring to a boil, reduce heat and simmer 5 minutes.

Remove from heat, cool and purée in batches in a blender, not a food processor, on high speed. Put through a strainer and return to pot. Bring to a boil and thicken slightly with a mixture of cornstarch dissolved in ¼ cup cold cream.

Over medium heat reduce the remaining 2 cups cream to 1 cup. Stir the reduced cream into the soup with the lemon juice and crème fraîche. Add salt and pepper to taste. Rewarm just before serving.

Smear 4 to 6 Tbsps. of garlic butter across the bottom of a sauté pan. Place oysters on top and slowly raise the heat, swirling the pan and just barely poaching the oysters.

In warmed soup bowls, place a dollop of garlic butter and 4 oysters. Ladle hot soup into bowls and garnish with arugula flowers.

Squab on Sage Pasta

Serves 6
Preparation Time: 25 Minutes

Sage Paparadelle Pasta

2½ cups all-purpose flour
1 tsp. salt
½ tsp. freshly ground black pepper
¼ cup sage leaves, dried, crumbled, tightly packed
4 eggs
3 egg yolk
2 Tbsps. olive oil

Mix all the dry ingredients together. Make a well in the center of the flour mixture. Set aside.

Lightly beat eggs, egg yolks and olive oil in a small mixing bowl. Pour into the well in the flour. Using a fork and in a swirling motion, gradually bring in the sides of the walls of the flour. When thickened enough, switch from the fork to your hands. Continue to work in the rest of the flour until you have achieved a malleable ball. Knead until the ball is smooth and elastic. A good test is to slice the ball in half and check for air bubbles. When they have vanished, you have a great pasta dough.

Roll dough as thinly as possible or run it through the rollers of a pasta machine.

Cut into paparadelle.

Cook the pasta in salted boiling water 3–4 minutes. Drain and serve with the squab and sauce.

Squab and Sauce

Serves 6
Preparation Time: One Hour

6 **whole squabs**
1 **medium onion, chopped**
1 **parsnip, peeled, chopped**
1 **carrot, peeled, chopped**
1 **bay leaf**
4 **sprigs fresh thyme or ½ tsp. dried**
12 **parsley stems**
2 **qts. veal stock**
   Salt and pepper
1 **cup red wine**
3 **Tbsps. butter, optional**
   Sage garnish, optional
   Roasted red pepper garnish, optional

   Remove the breasts, legs, thighs and wings from the squab. Trim the breasts of excess fat and skin. Reserve the legs and thighs for another meal. Reserve wings for sauce.
   To prepare the squab stock, place the squab carcasses in a 6 qt. stock pot with the onion, parsnip, carrot, bay leaf, thyme and parsley. Cover with the veal stock and simmer for 45 minutes. Strain. (The purpose of using veal stock is to give a doubly rich flavor to your sauce).
   Cut off the tip of the wings and discard. Brown the remaining wings in fat or oil and strain, removing the oil. To the browned wings add 3 to 4 cups squab stock and deglaze. Reduce the stock to a rich, thick glaze on the bottom of the pan. Add the remaining stock and reduce again until it coats the back of a spoon.
   Reduce the wine in half and add to the stock sauce, tasting as you go to reach a perfect acid level. Whisk in the butter. Season with salt and pepper. Strain and set aside.
   Heat a cast iron skillet and add clarified butter or oil and sear squab breasts, skin side down, for 2 minutes. Turn, salt and pepper seared skin and continue cooking 2 more minutes.
   To serve, place pasta in the center of a plate and top with the sliced squab breasts. Drizzle with the squab sauce and garnish with a sage sprig and/or diced roasted red peppers.

Raspberry Amaretto Custard Tarts

Serves 6
Preparation Time: 45 Minutes (note refrigeration time)
Pre-heat oven to 425°

Crust

1 cup flour
⅓ tsp. salt
2 Tbsps. sugar
6 Tbsps. butter

3 Tbsps. ice water
Beans or rice
to weigh down tarts

Place flour, salt and sugar in a mixing bowl. Cut in the butter and mix until mixture is coarse crumbs. Make a well in the center of the mixture and add the water. Bring flour in from the sides and very gently mix. Gather into a mound and chill about 2 hours.

Roll out dough and cut to fit individual tart tins. Fit pastry into tins and press firmly against bottom and side. Prick with a fork. Chill. Fit pastry with foil and fill in with beans or rice. Bake 12 to 15 minutes. Remove foil and beans and continue baking if necessary to a light golden brown.

Amaretto Custard

2 cups milk
¾ cup sugar
½ cup flour
⅛ tsp. salt
2 egg yolks, beaten

5 Tbsps. butter
1 tsp. vanilla
¼ cup Amaretto
1 jar apricot jam
Raspberries

Scald milk. Mix the sugar, flour and salt. Add to hot milk and cook until thick. Add beaten egg yolks and continue cooking for 3 minutes, beating constantly. Stir in butter, vanilla and Amaretto. Allow to cool.

Melt jam in a saucepan and put through a fine sieve.

Put a small layer of custard in the bottom of each tart shell. Fill with raspberries and glaze with melted jam.

99

DEPOT 1870 RESTAURANT

NORTHERN ITALIAN
241 First Street West
Sonoma
938-2980
Lunch Wednesday–Friday 11:30AM–2PM
Dinner Wednesday–Sunday from 5PM on
AVERAGE DINNER FOR TWO: $30

THE DEPOT 1870 restaurant is housed in an historic building a block off the Plaza in Sonoma. Built with stones from General Vallejo's quarries, the original owners opened the building as a hotel and restaurant serving Italian dinners to the train passengers and the town of Sonoma. After many subsequent years as a private home followed by extensive restoration, the Depot 1870 Restaurant is now a haven for fans of Northern Italian food.

The atmosphere is cozy, romantic and relaxed. Award-winning Northern Italian cuisine by Chef-owner Michael Ghilarducci emphasizes subtle sauces and fresh local products. The menu he has designed offers a large selection of Tuscan specialties—particularly the fragrant homemade pastas and risottos that delight all the senses. Range-fed veal, house-aged beef and a wide variety of fresh seafood round out the menu. In addition to a selection of Italian ice creams, delicious Italian desserts such as Tiramisu and Bacardi Rum Cake are made by the chef's wife, Gia.

Buon appetitio!

DEPOT HOTEL 1870
RESTAURANT
AND
WINE BAR

100

Prawns with White Beans (Gamberoni e Fagioli)

Serves Four
Preparation Time: 2 Hours

  1 **cup cannellini (dry white beans)**
1¼ **lbs. prawns**
  2 **tomatoes, skinned, seeded, chopped**
  6 **fresh basil leaves, chopped coarse**
 ½ **cup extra virgin olive oil**
    Salt and pepper

Cook the beans in boiling salted water until tender, about 2 hours.

Drop the prawns into a saucepan of boiling salted water. Cook 5 minutes. Shell the prawns as soon as they have cooled enough to touch.

Combine the prawns with the drained beans, tomatoes and basil. Toss with olive oil and season lightly with salt and pepper.

Serve warm.

Fresh Spinach Pasta
with Meat Sauce
(Tagliarini al Verde Bolognese)

Serves 4
Preparation Time: 2 Hours

1¼ cups cooked spinach, drained	½ tsp. olive oil
2 whole eggs	2 cups flour
	½ tsp. salt

Purée spinach very fine in a food processor. Add eggs and oil and mix again. In a mixing bowl with a dough hook, blend flour and salt. Add the spinach mixture to the dry ingredients and knead well until shiny and elastic. Cover with plastic and let rest at least 45 minutes.

Meanwhile make the Bolognese Sauce, below. When dough has rested, roll out into a thin sheet. Pass through a pasta machine to make tagliarini or roll dough up jelly-roll fashion and cut with a sharp knife. Toss with flour and cover with plastic until ready to cook.

When Bolognese Sauce is ready and warm, drop the pasta into rapidly boiling salted water. Cook 2 minutes, drain, place on platter and top with sauce.

Bolognese Sauce

½ lb. ground beef	1 can diced tomatoes
½ lb. ground veal	in purée (29 oz.)
½ lb. ground pork	1 tsp. basil
2 Tbsps. olive oil	1 tsp. oregano
1 large onion, chopped	1 tsp. sage
6 cloves garlic, finely chopped	½ tsp. thyme
1 cup red wine	

Sauté ground meats in olive oil until brown. Add the onion and garlic, sauté lightly. Add red wine and cook over moderate heat until liquid has reduced by half. Add the tomatoes and herbs and cook over medium-low heat for about 45 minutes more.

Use about 1 cup of the finished sauce per person to go over pasta. The rest of the sauce may be kept for up to a week in the refrigerator.

Cauliflower Salad
(Insalata di Rinforzo)

Serves 4
Preparation Time: 15 Minutes (note refrigeration time)

1 cauliflower
  Salt
⅓ cup green olives, pitted, halved
⅓ cup black olives, pitted, halved
⅓ cup sweet gherkin pickles, chopped
⅓ cup pimentos, chopped
6 anchovy filets, drained, chopped
1 Tbsp. capers
6 Tbsps. olive oil
1 Tbsp. vinegar
  Freshly ground black pepper

Divide cauliflower into small flowerets and cook in boiling salted water for about 5 minutes. Flowerets should remain crisp. Drain and chill.

When cold, place in bowl with olives, gherkins, pimentos, anchovies and capers. Add olive oil, vinegar, salt and pepper. Toss gently to mix and chill at least 30 minutes before serving.

Cooking tip: Blanched red bell peppers can be substituted for pimentos.

Scallops of Veal
with Prosciutto & Sage
(Vitello Saltimbocca)

Serves 4
Preparation Time: 15 Minutes

1½ lbs. scallops of veal
 2 Tbsps. olive oil
    Flour
12 fresh sage leaves
12 prosciutto slices, paper thin
 2 Tbsps. shallots
½ cup Marsala
½ cup veal demi-glace
 1 Tbsp. sweet butter

    Cut veal into 2 oz. strips and pound flat.

    Heat oil in a large sauté pan. Dredge veal lightly in flour and dust off all excess. Sauté over high heat for 1 minute on first side. Turn veal and top with sage and prosciutto. Add shallots and sauté for 1 minute. Add Marsala and remove the veal to the plates or serving platter.

    Reduce liquid in pan by half. Add demi-glace and bring back up to a simmer. Swirl in butter and pour over veal.

Soufflé Cake of Walnuts & Almonds with Mocha and Cappuccino Buttercreams (Cassata Moka)

Serves 4
Preparation Time: 2 Hours; Pre-heat oven to 350°

8 whole eggs, separated
¾ cups sugar
2 Tbsps. bread crumbs
2 Tbsps. rum

1 cup walnuts, finely ground
1 cup almonds, finely ground
⅛ tsp. cream of tartar

Butter and flour a 10″ springform pan. Beat the egg yolks until very light. Add sugar and mix until thick and yellow. Soak bread crumbs in rum and add to the egg mixture along with the ground nuts. Beat the whites until stiff, with the cream of tartar. Fold in whites and blend well. Bake at 350° for 45 minutes. Cool on rack.

Mocha & Cappuccino Buttercreams

8 egg yolks
4 Tbsps. sugar
4 Tbsps. flour
2½ cups milk, scalding
1 tsp. vanilla
2 Tbsps. rum

3 cubes sweet butter
2 lbs. powdered sugar
3 Tbsps. instant coffee
¼ cup dark chocolate, melted
Chocolate-covered
espresso beans

Prepare the cream filling by beating 4 egg yolks hard with sugar and flour in a saucepan until thick and yellow. Slowly pour in scalding milk and cook over medium heat, stirring constantly until it has thickened and coats a wooden spoon. Reduce heat to low and add vanilla and rum. Cook another 5 minutes until quite thick. Pour into a bowl, cover the surface with a piece of plastic and chill thoroughly.

Prepare the buttercream frosting by beating the butter until fluffy. Add the powdered sugar and beat high until smooth. Beat in the yolks. Dissolve the instant coffee in ½ cup hot water, then cool. Slowly add to the butter mixture. Add the melted chocolate and place in a pastry bag with a star tip.

Slice cake in half and put the bottom half on a serving platter, cut side up. Cover with the refrigerated cream filling. Top with cake layer and frost with Cappuccino buttercream. Garnish with chocolate-covered espresso beans.

GLEN ELLEN INN

CALIFORNIA CUISINE
13670 Arnold Drive
Glen Ellen
996-6409
Dinner by reservation only
Wednesday–Sunday from 6PM
AVERAGE DINNER FOR TWO: $40

THIS TINY RESTAURANT is easy to miss. Set in a cozy cottage on Glen Ellen's main street, the Glen Ellen Inn looks like someone's home. With only nine tables there is just enough room for 22 diners.

Bob and Lynda Rice have operated this intimate eatery in the Sonoma Valley for the past five years and have developed a loyal following of customers drawn to their warm hospitality and creative cookery. Chef Bob Rice prepares dishes that are elegant in appearance and emphasize strong Mediterranean flavors. He shops each morning, selecting meat, fish and poultry and visiting local farms for organically grown produce.

The small handwritten menu changes nightly and offers a choice of several appetizers, three entrees, a special salad and two or three desserts.

GLEN ELLEN INN

Chef Bob Rice's Menu for Four

Roasted Eggplant & Red Onion Soup
Bruschetta with Marinated Goat Cheese
Grilled Swordfish with Stewed Garlic, Artichokes & Aioli
Lemon Tart

Roasted Eggplant & Red Onion Soup

Serves 4
Preparation Time: 1½ Hours
Pre-heat oven to 350°

2 lbs. eggplant
2 medium red onions
2 cloves garlic
Olive oil
Salt and pepper
1 qt. chicken stock

Rub eggplant, red onion and garlic lightly with olive oil and roast in a 350° oven until eggplant is soft and has begun to collapse, about 1 hour. Cool and peel the eggplant and red onions and roughly chop.

In a large saucepan, stew the chopped eggplant, red onions and garlic in 4 Tbsps. olive oil over low heat for 15 minutes. The vegetables should be very soft. Season with salt and pepper and cover with chicken stock. Cook for 10 minutes.

Purée the soup in a blender and adjust the seasonings before serving.

Bruschetta with Marinated Goat Cheese

Serves 4
Preparation Time: 20 Minutes (note marinating time)

¾ lb. goat cheese
   Extra virgin olive oil
 2 tsps. fresh thyme leaves
 2 cloves garlic, sliced thin
¼ tsp. coarsely ground black pepper
 1 onion, chopped
 2 large sweet red peppers, charred, peeled, julienned
 2 tomatoes, peeled, seeded, chopped
 2 Tbsps. currants
¼ cup sherry vinegar
¼ tsp. red pepper flakes
½ tsp. salt
 2 Tbsps. chopped fresh basil
 8 thick slices crusty sourdough or country bread

Place goat cheese in a small bowl and cover with olive oil, thyme leaves, garlic and black pepper to marinate.

Heat 3 Tbsps. olive oil in a pan over medium heat and sauté the onions until soft. Add red peppers, tomatoes, currants, sherry vinegar, red pepper flakes and salt. Simmer gently for a few minutes to blend the flavors. Stir in basil.

To serve, fry the bread slices in hot olive oil or grill them until they are crispy. Spread with the marinated goat cheese and top with the red pepper mixture. Serve immediately.

Grilled Swordfish with Stewed Garlic, Artichokes & Aioli

Serves Four
Preparation Time: 1 Hour

  20 small artichokes
     Extra virgin olive oil
  16 cloves garlic, peeled
   2 tsps. fresh thyme
1¼ cups white wine
     Salt and pepper
   4 swordfish steaks, 1″ thick

Pull off the tough outer leaves of the artichokes and pare the artichoke down to the tender part of leaves and heart.

Heat some olive oil in a pan and sauté the chokes for a few minutes. Add the whole garlic cloves and the thyme and sauté a few minutes more. Add the white wine and gently simmer for 1 hour or until the garlic is tender. Salt and pepper to taste.

Grill the swordfish steaks over high heat for about 3 minutes per side. The steaks are best seared on the outside and just cooked through. Take care not to overcook them or they will taste very dry.

Spoon the artichokes and garlic over the swordfish and drizzle with some of the aioli. (See following recipe.)

Cooking tip: Serve with baby red potatoes, oven roasted with fennel seed, salt and olive oil.

Aioli

Preparation Time: 5 Minutes

   1 **Tbsp. garlic, minced**
   3 **egg yolks**
   2 **Tbsps. fresh lemon juice**
   ½ **tsp. salt**
1½ **cups extra virgin olive oil**

   In a food processor, combine the garlic, egg yolks, lemon juice and salt.
   With the motor running, slowly add the olive oil until thick.

Lemon Tart

Preparation Time: 1 Hour, 15 Minutes
Pre-heat oven to 350°

1½ cubes cold sweet butter
⅓ cup powdered sugar
1¾ cups flour
4 eggs
2 cups sugar
1 tsp. baking powder
2 lemons, zest and juice
   Whipped cream garnish

In a food processor, make the dough by blending the butter, powdered sugar and 1½ cups flour. Press dough into a 10" removable
bottom tart pan and bake until slightly browned, about 20 to 30 minutes. Cool.

In a mixing bowl, combine the eggs, sugar, 4 Tbsps. flour, baking
powder and lemons. Fill the cooled tart shell.

Bake at 350° until just set, about 30 minutes.

Cool and dust with powdered sugar. Serve with softly whipped
cream.

111

THE GRILLE
SONOMA MISSION INN & SPA

WINE COUNTRY CUISINE
18140 Sonoma Highway 12
Boyes Hot Springs
938-9000
Lunch 11:30AM–2:30PM
Dinner 6PM–10PM
Sunday Brunch 10AM–2PM
AVERAGE DINNER FOR TWO: $75

THE SONOMA MISSION Inn and Spa is a luxury resort and European-style spa surrounded by eight acres of eucalyptus-shaded grounds. The rambling California mission style building, constructed in 1927, has a history rich in the colorful lore of the Sonoma Valley. The Boyes Hot Springs site was originally used as a sacred healing ground by indigenous Indians who were drawn by the curative powers of its underground springs.

Today, Sonoma Mission Inn is noted for its state-of-the-art facilities, including a complete bathhouse, exercise equipment, pool and beauty salon. Famed for its innovative gourmet meals, the spa attracts an international clientele and has generated a cookbook, "Spa Food," published by Clarkson N. Potter, a division of Crown Publishers.

The Grille features a seasonal menu of Wine Country Cuisine prepared exclusively with fresh, locally grown products. Spa Cuisine is also available at lunch and dinner, featuring innovative dishes which are lower in calories, sodium and cholesterol. An international wine list features over 200 premium selections from Sonoma and Napa counties.

Chef Michael Flynn's Menu for Four

Apple, Pear & Arugula Salad
with Balsamic Vinaigrette

Roast Salmon on Warm Niçoise Vegetables
with Basil Pesto

Classic Crème Brulée

Apple, Pear & Arugula Salad with Balsamic Vinaigrette

Serves 4
Preparation Time: 15 Minutes

  4 **bunches arugula**
  2 **apples, sliced**
  2 **pears, sliced**
 ¼ **cup walnuts, toasted**
  1 **shallot, minced**
  1 **clove garlic, minced**
 ⅓ **cup balsamic vinegar**
 ½ **cup olive oil**
    Salt and pepper to taste
  1 **tsp. lemon juice**
 ¼ **lb. Gorgonzola cheese**

Remove stems, wash and dry arugula. Place in bowl with apples, pears and nuts.

Prepare the balsamic vinaigrette by combining the shallot, garlic, balsamic vinegar, olive oil, salt, pepper and lemon juice. Whisk vigorously until blended.

Toss the salad with the vinaigrette and place on 4 chilled plates. Crumble Gorgonzola on each.

Roast Salmon on Warm Niçoise Vegetables with Basil Pesto

Serves 4
Preparation Time: 30 Minutes

2 bunches basil
3 cloves garlic
1 tsp. pine nuts
⅓ cup olive oil
1 Tbsp. Parmesan cheese, grated
2 Tbsps. lemon juice
   Salt and pepper to taste
4 salmon steaks
½ lb. green beans, blanched, sliced
2 russet potatoes, peeled, diced, blanched
2 tomatoes, peeled, seeded, diced
¼ cup Niçoise olives, pitted
2 Tbsps. capers

Prepare the basil pesto by combining the basil, 2 cloves garlic and pine nuts in a food processor and purée. Add olive oil to form a paste. Add cheese, 1 Tbsp. lemon juice, salt and pepper. Set aside.

In a hot saucepan, add 3 Tbsps. olive oil. Season salmon steaks with salt and pepper and sear on both sides until golden brown. Then place salmon in 350° oven until cooked to desired doneness.

Add 2 Tbsps. olive oil to saucepan and sauté 2 tsps. garlic for 30 seconds. Add beans and potatoes and cook for 2 minutes. Add tomatoes, olives, capers, salt, pepper, and 1 Tbsp. lemon juice, cooking for 1 minute.

Divide vegetables evenly between warmed plates. Remove salmon from oven and place in center, atop vegetables. Top with basil pesto and grated Parmesan.

Classic Crème Brulée

Serves 4
Preparation Time: 2½ Hours (note refrigeration time)
Pre-heat oven to 325°

7 egg yolks
⅔ cup sugar
6 Tbsps. vanilla extract
2⅔ cups whipping cream
1 cup brown sugar

Mix together with wire whip the yolks, sugar, and vanilla until smooth. Add cream and mix until smooth. Try to incorporate as little air as possible by mixing with short strokes.

Put into 1 cup oven-proof individual serving dishes. Place these cups into a larger, deeper pan, also oven-proof. Fill larger pan with enough water to reach half way up the sides of the cups. Place in 325° oven and bake for 2 hours. Test the cups by shaking them gently. They should be firm and well set but not solid.

Remove from oven, cool in the larger pan for 30 minutes. Remove from pan and cool overnight in refrigerator.

Before serving, sprinkle brown sugar over each and caramelize under broiler.

JOHN ASH & CO.

CALIFORNIA CUISINE
4330 Barnes Road
Santa Rosa
527-7687
Lunch Tuesday–Friday 11:30AM–2PM
Dinner Tuesday–Sunday 5:30PM–9:30PM
Sunday Brunch 10:30AM–2PM
AVERAGE DINNER FOR TWO: $60

JOHN ASH & CO. aspires to be the showplace for Sonoma County food and wines. The cuisine is purely "John Ash," a style that defies definition but incorporates the influences of French, Latin America, the Southwest and the Orient. The menu focuses on regional fresh foods.

The restaurant reflects the Provençal style of Southern France and accommodates guests in the elegance of two dining rooms where French windows allow the landscape of the surrounding vineyards to become part of the decor. On a warm day, diners may prefer the view of the distant mountains and a glass of wine on the trellised outdoor patio. In the evening, the inviting lounge provides a casual meeting place to enjoy the glow of the fireplace.

Since its founding ten years ago, the restaurant has gathered numerous awards and accolades. It was recently named "One of the Top 50 Restaurants in the Country" by the Condé Nast Traveler. It has also been named as having a "Best Restaurant Wine List" for the past eight years by The Wine Spectator.

Warm Salad of Winter Greens with Pancetta
Grilled Polenta with Sonoma Jack Cheese
Poached Pears with Ginger Crème Anglaise

Warm Salad of Winter Greens with Pancetta

Serves 6
Preparation Time: 15 Minutes

6 cups salad greens
6 thin slices pancetta
6 Tbsps. walnut oil
4 Tbsps. raspberry vinegar
2 Tbsps. honey
2 Tbsps. pine nuts, toasted
Chrysanthemum petals, garnish (optional)

Wash greens thoroughly and tear into serving-size pieces.

Sauté pancetta in a nonstick skillet until lightly cooked, about 3 minutes, drain and keep warm.

In a large skillet, heat the walnut oil, vinegar and honey. Add greens and stir for a few seconds, until slightly wilted. Do not overcook.

Serve on warmed plates garnished with pancetta, pine nuts and chrysanthemum petals, if used.

Cooking tip: Use a combination of greens such as mustard, kale, spinach, endive and radicchio.

Grilled Polenta
with Sonoma Jack Cheese

Serves 6
Preparation Time: 45 Minutes (note refrigeration time)

1 qt. chicken stock or chicken broth
  Salt and white pepper
2 tsps. ground white pepper
1 tsp. fresh thyme, minced
1 cup polenta or yellow cornmeal
8 Tbsps. (1 stick) butter
½ cup mushrooms, minced
½ cup scallions, minced
½ cup dry white wine
1 Tbsp. parsley, minced
½ lb. Sonoma jack cheese, sliced
⅓ lb. shiitake mushrooms, sliced
2 Tbsps. sun-dried tomatoes, sliced

In a large saucepan, bring stock, salt to taste, white pepper and thyme to a boil. Slowly stir in polenta or cornmeal with a whisk to avoid lumps. Reduce heat to low and stir to prevent sticking. Cook slowly for 10 minutes.

In a separate skillet, heat 2 Tbsps. butter. Sauté minced mushrooms and scallions until brown, about 5 minutes. Season with salt and pepper. Add wine and reduce until most of the wine cooks away. Add to polenta mixture with remaining butter and parsley.

Butter a large shallow dish or baking sheet. Spread polenta mixture in the dish to a depth of ½" and smooth top. Cool, cover with plastic wrap and refrigerate.

Cut polenta into 4" diamonds. Grill until surface is lightly toasted. Turn, cover with a slice of jack cheese and grill until cheese is just starting to melt.

Sauté the shiitake mushrooms in butter.

Serve the grilled polenta warm, garnished with the shiitake mushrooms and slivers of sun-dried tomatoes.

Poached Pears
with Ginger Crème Anglaise

Serves 6
Preparation Time: 45 Minutes

6 firm pears
2½ cups white wine
1½ cups sugar
1 3-inch piece lemon zest
2 vanilla beans, split or 1 tsp. vanilla extract
½ cup mascarpone
¼ cup ginger root, peeled, chopped
¼ cup water
2 cups half and half
5 large egg yolks

Peel pears, leaving stems on, and core from underneath. In a saucepan just large enough to hold pears upright, combine wine, 1 cup sugar, lemon zest and 1 vanilla bean or ½ tsp. vanilla extract. Bring to a boil and simmer for 5 minutes. Add pears and poach for 10 minutes or until cooked through. A toothpick should pierce them easily. Allow pears to cool in the poaching liquid. Drain and stuff core cavity with mascarpone.

Prepare the ginger crème anglaise by placing the ginger, 2 Tbsps. sugar and water in a heavy-bottomed saucepan. Simmer until syrup becomes very thick, about 10 minutes. Do not allow syrup to turn color and caramelize. Add half and half and vanilla bean or vanilla extract and bring to a boil. Remove from heat and let stand for 30 minutes.

Beat egg yolks with remaining sugar. Reheat cream mixture to simmering point and whisk into egg yolk mixture. Return entire mixture to pan and cook, stirring constantly, until thickened. Fill a large bowl with shaved ice and set a second bowl within it. Strain the custard into this bowl and cool, stirring occasionally.

To serve, pour a pool of crème anglaise onto each dessert plate. Top with a poached stuffed pear.

119

La Gare

FRENCH CONTINENTAL
208 Wilson Street
Santa Rosa
528-4355
Dinner Tuesday–Sunday 5:30PM–10PM
AVERAGE DINNER FOR TWO: $30

La GARE, LOCATED in Santa Rosa's historic Railroad Square, has retained its popularity over the years. Voted Sonoma County's most romantic restaurant, La Gare creates a quiet intimate atmosphere, offering a true adventure in hospitality.

The authentic French kitchen presents specialties such as chateaubriand bouquetiere for two, braised duck in orange sauce, raspberries flambé and chocolate decadence.

An evening at La Gare is a blend of impeccable service, superb cuisine and great wine.

Chef Roger Praplan's Menu for Four

La Gare Salad Dressing
Halibut in Champagne Sauce
Chocolate Decadence

La Gare Salad Dressing

Yields 4 cups
Preparation Time: 10 Minutes

2 egg yolks
1 Tbsp. Dijon mustard
1 Tbsp. Worcestershire sauce
1 Tbsp. lemon juice
½ tsp. salt
½ tsp. white pepper
1 qt. oil of your choice

In a blender, combine the egg yolks, mustard, Worcestershire sauce, lemon juice, salt and pepper. Slowly add the oil until the salad dressing is thick and creamy.

If the dressing becomes too thick, add lukewarm water to bring to desired consistency.

Cooking tip: After washing lettuce, add a few drops of white wine vinegar. This will flush out any small bugs and also render the lettuce more crisp.

Halibut in Champagne Sauce

Serves 4
Preparation Time: 30 Minutes

   4 **halibut filets, 6 oz. each**
      Salt and white pepper
 ½ **tsp. shallots, minced**
 ½ **Tbsp. tomato sauce or paste**
 ¼ **cup fish stock, optional**
 ¼ **cup champagne**
 ½ **cup heavy cream**

    Salt and pepper bottom side of the halibut and place in a buttered pan over medium heat. Add the shallots, tomato paste, fish stock, champagne and the cream. Bring to a boil and cover with a lid or buttered parchment paper, to keep the fish from drying out. Cook until the fish is firm.

    Remove fish and reduce the sauce to desired consistency.

    Serve halibut drizzled with champagne sauce.

Chocolate Decadence

Yields: One 8″ cake pan or mold
Serves 10–12 portions
Preparation Time: 30 Minutes
Pre-Heat oven to 350°

6 whole eggs
3 egg yolks
1 Tbsp. sugar
1 Tbsp. flour
½ lb. bittersweet chocolate
½ lb. dark sweet chocolate
10 Tbsps. (1¼ sticks) butter
Raspberry sauce for garnish

In a mixing bowl, blend the whole eggs, egg yolks, sugar and flour until smooth and thick. Set aside.

In a double boiler, melt the bittersweet and dark sweet chocolate with the butter. Slowly add the egg mixture until incorporated.

Pour into a mold and bake at 350° for 12 to 14 minutes. Cool before serving.

To serve, slice using a warm knife, cleaning it every time you slice. Place a piece of chocolate decadence on a cold plate with raspberry sauce.

Cooking tip: Chocolate decadence can be frozen after it cools.

LES ARCADES

FRENCH
133 East Napa
Sonoma
938-3723
Wednesday–Sunday 5PM–10PM
AVERAGE DINNER FOR TWO: $60

LES ARCADES, A country French restaurant, continues to earn extraordinary acclaim. The menu is innovative and trendy, offering an elegant dining experience.

Here, guests enjoy superb French cuisine, fine wines and an ambiance graced by soft lighting, hand-carved woods and etched glass. Firelight greetings await you in the dining room and outdoor patio.

Chef Dominique Leiseing's Menu for Four

Oyster Ragout on Watercress
Halibut with Eggplant in Basil Sauce
Chocolate Mousse Squares

Oyster Ragout on Watercress

Serves 4
Preparation Time: 15 Minutes

16 fresh oysters
½ cup white wine
**   Pinch of cayenne pepper**
3 Tbsps. shallots, minced
½ tsp. white peppercorns, crushed
3 Tbsps. white wine vinegar
¾ cup cold butter, unsalted, sliced small
2 qts. water
½ tsp. salt
1 bunch watercress, trimmed

Remove shells from oysters, saving the liquid. In a small saucepan, combine the oysters, reserved liquid and ¼ cup wine. Set aside.

Prepare the sauce by combing the shallots, ¼ cup wine, white peppercorns and vinegar over low heat. Add the butter and cook, whisking constantly until creamy. Strain and keep warm.

Bring water to a boil and add salt. Blanch watercress for 3 minutes and cool in ice water. Drain and place in blender. Process until puréed. Add sauce and process until watercress has a thick mousse-like texture.

To serve, heat oysters over low heat until liquid begins to bubble. Divide watercress among 4 hot plates. Top with oysters.

Halibut with Eggplant

Serves 4
Preparation Time: 45 Minutes
Pre-heat oven to 350°

4 halibut or sea bass filets	2 Tbsps. shallots, minced
5 small Japanese eggplants	½ cup white wine
2 Tbsps. olive oil	½ cup chicken stock
2 Tbsps. onion, chopped fine	¼ tsp. soy sauce
¼ tsp. garlic, minced	Zest of 1 lemon, grated
½ tsp. walnut oil	¼ tsp. lemon juice
2 Tbsps. red pepper, diced	12 large fresh basil leaves,
9 Tbsps. unsalted butter	julienned
2 large potatoes, boiled,	
cut into 16 slices	

Cut 4 eggplants in half. Scoop out centers, chop and set aside. Blanch the eggplant halves in boiling salted water for 5 minutes. Remove and place in an oven-proof dish. Peel and dice the fifth eggplant. Cook the diced eggplant and reserved eggplant flesh in boiling water for 2 minutes. Remove and drain.

In a heavy saucepan, heat 1 Tbsp. olive oil and sauté the onion. Add the eggplant pieces, garlic, walnut oil and red pepper. Cook over medium heat for 5 minutes. Spoon mixture into four of the eggplant halves. Place the 8 eggplant halves and potatoes in 350° oven. Bake for 8–10 minutes.

In a large skillet, heat 1 Tbsp. olive oil and 2 Tbsps. butter, sauté the fish filets for 3 minutes on each side or until cooked.

Prepare the basil sauce by combining the shallots and wine over medium heat until reduced to a few tablespoons. Add chicken stock, soy sauce and grated lemon zest, cooking over medium heat until reduced by half. Whisk in 7 Tbsps. butter, a few pieces at a time. Add lemon juice and basil.

To serve, place fish filet in the center of each heated plate. Garnish plate with a filled eggplant and cover with an empty eggplant half. Arrange potato slices and drizzle with the basil sauce.

Chocolate Mousse Squares

Serves 6
Preparation Time: 1 Hour (note refrigeration time)

½ lb. semisweet chocolate
   Parchment paper
5 Tbsps. unsalted butter
½ cup unsweetened cocoa
2 egg yolks
¼ cup sugar
2 Tbsps. strong coffee
2 Tbsps. water
½ cup heavy cream, whipped firm

In a double boiler, melt ¼ lb. semisweet chocolate. Remove from heat and cool. Place an 8"x10" piece of parchment paper on a cookie sheet and pour melted chocolate into center. Spread with a spatula and set aside to harden. Do not refrigerate. When chocolate has hardened, score 12 rectangles.

Prepare the chocolate mousse by combining the butter, ¼ lb. semisweet chocolate and cocoa in a double boiler until melted and thoroughly combined. Remove from heat.

With an electric mixer, beat the egg yolks and sugar until pale and thick. Beat in coffee and water. Slowly add the warmed chocolate mixture. Beat in whipped cream. Cover and refrigerate for at least 2 hours.

To serve, carefully peel chocolate rectangles from parchment paper. Place a chocolate rectangle on each plate, top with a large dollop of chocolate mousse and cover with remaining rectangles.

L'ESPERANCE

FRENCH
464 1st Street East
Sonoma
996-2757
Lunch and dinner daily
Sunday brunch
AVERAGE DINNER FOR TWO: $50

L'ESPERANCE CREATES AN elegant mood with a menu to match. Noted for true and simple contemporary French cuisine, owner Bob Subaie uses only the best produce, meats and seafood. The food is fresh, the portions generous.

House delicacies include seared sea scallops arranged around a mound of snow peas and baby anise, dressed in a lime vinaigrette. Other goodies include salmon in warm tomato herb sauce and duck roasted with honey, lemon and cumin. The walnut torte is a wedge of solid praline atop a dense crust, then drizzled with crème anglaise and raspberry purée.

The service is refined and courteous, yet personal and knowledgeable. The atmosphere is as elegant as the service, with added touches of fresh flowers, crisp linen and soft music.

L'Esperance is one of the best French restaurants in California. It is a place for unhurried dining and quiet conversation in an intimate atmosphere.

128

Chef Bob Subaie's Menu for Four

Cream of Anise Soup
Grilled Shiitake Salad
Salmon in Warm Tomato Herb Sauce

Cream of Anise Soup

Serves 8
Preparation Time: 25 Minutes

  1 **carrot, peeled**
  1 **medium white onion**
  2 **stalks celery**
  2 **Tbsps. olive oil**
  2 **qts. chicken broth**
  4 **stalks anise, chopped**
1½ **cups heavy cream**
  ¼ **tsp. ground nutmeg**
     Salt and pepper to taste

Cut the carrot, onion and celery into 1" pieces. Combine in a 5 qt. pot and sauté lightly in olive oil.

Add the chicken broth and bring to a boil. Add the anise and simmer until all ingredients are semi-soft.

Remove from heat, cool slightly and strain. Replace in pot and add cream to desired taste. Add nutmeg, salt and pepper and bring to a boil. Immediately reduce the heat and simmer for 5 minutes before serving.

Grilled Shiitake Salad

Serves 4
Preparation Time: 20 Minutes

  8 large shiitake mushrooms
¾ cup olive oil
  1 Tbsp. garlic, minced
     Salt and pepper to taste
  8 tsps. pesto sauce
  8 slices of pepper jack cheese
¼ cup balsamic vinegar
¼ cup red wine vinegar
  1 lb. baby green salad mix

Clean and core shiitake mushrooms. Brush with olive oil and minced garlic. Sprinkle with salt and pepper to taste.

Grill lightly, about 30 seconds per side. Remove and stuff with 1 tsp. pesto per mushroom. Place on a baking sheet and cover with a slice of pepper jack cheese. Broil until cheese melts.

Prepare the dressing by combining ½ cup olive oil, balsamic vinegar and red wine vinegar in a bowl. Mix vigorously with a spoon or fork. Do not blend.

Cover each plate with baby greens. Place 2 grilled shiitakes in center of each plate. Sprinkle dressing to taste over top.

Salmon in Warm Tomato Herb Sauce

Serves 4
Preparation Time: 15 Minutes
Pre-heat oven to 450°

   4 **salmon filets, 6 oz. each**
     Salt and pepper to taste
   4 **large tomatoes, peeled, seeded**
   2 **bunches fresh basil leaves**
   4 **shallots**
   1 **tsp. whole coriander**
     Juice of half lemon
 ¾ **cup olive oil**

   Salt and pepper salmon, then rub the filets with about ¼ cup
olive oil. Oil a baking pan and roast salmon at 450° for 8–10 minutes.
   In a food processor or blender, combine the tomatoes, basil, shallots, coriander, lemon juice and ½ cup olive oil. Blend until chunky.
Do not cook.
   To serve, preheat serving plate. The plate should be hot to the
touch, as the plate serves as the "warmer" for the sauce. Place uncooked sauce on hot dishes. Place salmon filet on top of warmed
sauce.

Cooking tip: Serve with boiled new potatoes and/or braised anise.
Garnish with fresh basil leaves.

LISA HEMENWAY'S

CALIFORNIA CUISINE
714 Village Court
Montgomery Village
Santa Rosa
526-5111
Lunch Monday–Saturday 11:30AM–2:30PM
Dinner Tuesday–Saturday 5:30PM–9:30PM
AVERAGE DINNER FOR TWO: $35

THE DELIGHTFULLY UNUSUAL and colorful array of California cuisine presented by Lisa Hemenway at her Santa Rosa restaurant has brought her recognition as one of the most honored chefs in Northern California. In 1989, Lisa was honored as the Outstanding Chef of the Year by the Sonoma Country Art Awards.

Lisa's artfully designed restaurant features epicurean delights including such innovative dishes as grilled vine leaves with chevre, Indonesian noodles, stuffed eggplant, lavosh and lots of fresh, Sonoma County fruits and vegetables. The desserts are already legendary.

Noted for her flair of presentation, Lisa believes that everything on the plate should be as delectable as it is attractive. Her blending of taste delights and color make each dish noteworthy and memorable.

Baked Pasta Putanesca in Parchment

Serves 4
Preparation Time: 30 Minutes
Pre-heat oven to 350°

¼ **cup sun-dried tomatoes**
4 **Tbsps. capers**
¼ **cup pitted Niçoise olives**
1 **tsp. garlic**
1 **tsp. chiles, crushed**
¼ **cup basil leaves, packed**
¼ **cup parsley leaves**
½ **cup Asiago cheese**
¾ **cup olive oil**
  Angel hair pasta
  Parchment paper

In a food processor, combine the tomatoes, capers, olive, garlic and chiles. Set aside. In the food processor, combine the basil, parsley, cheese and olive oil.

In a bowl, blend all the ingredients to make the sauce. Do not heat. Set aside

Blanch the angel hair pasta in boiling water. Drain and toss in the sauce. Take an 11 x 18-inch piece of parchment and wrap pasta up like a beggar's purse and tie with a ribbon. Bake for 12 minutes at 350.°

Cooking tip: Serve with vegetable confetti (carrots, cabbage and red peppers chopped small.)

Mixed Greens with Fig, Prosciutto & Chèvre

Preparation Time: 30 Minutes

- 1 garlic clove, minced
- 1 Tbsp. salt
- 4 Tbsps. lemon juice
- 2 Tbsps. red wine
- 1 tsp. white pepper
- 1 Tbsp. Dijon mustard
- ¾ cup walnut oil
- 4 cups mixed greens
- 4 slices prosciutto
- 1½ cups walnuts
- 8 black fig slices for garnish
- 2 Tbsps. goat cheese for garnish

To make the walnut dressing, blend garlic, salt, lemon, red wine, pepper and Dijon mustard. Whisk in the walnut oil.

Toss 1 handful of greens per person and coat lightly with the walnut dressing. Lay a ribbon of prosciutto over the top.

Garnish with walnuts, fig slices and crumbled goat cheese.

Lamb Tenderloins Sauté

Serves 4
Preparation Time: 20 Minutes

12 **tenderloins of lamb, 3 per person**
 1 **cup flour**
   Salt and pepper
 3 **Tbsps. vegetable oil or clarified butter**
 2 **Tbsps. shallots, minced**
⅓ **cup balsamic vinegar**
½ **cup veal stock**
 2 **Tbsps. Mendocino sweet mustard**
¼ **cup hazelnuts, toasted**

Clean fat and sinew from tenderloins. Dredge in flour, salt and pepper. Sauté in vegetable oil or clarified butter. Sear both sides on high heat. These cook quickly.

When lamb is browned, drain excess oil and add shallots. Glaze pan with balsamic vinegar. Add stock and sweet mustard. Reduce heat and add hazelnuts.

Place lamb on serving dish and pour sauce over it.

MADRONA MANOR

CALIFORNIA CUISINE
1001 Westside Road
Healdsburg
433-4433
Dinner nightly 6PM–9PM
Sunday Brunch 11AM–2PM
AVERAGE DINNER FOR TWO: $70

DINING AT MADRONA Manor is a memorable experience. The chef-owner Todd Muir, is a graduate of the California Culinary Academy and worked at Alice Waters' famed Chez Panisse Restaurant in Berkeley. Muir composes menus that elevate to prominence the finest fresh produce and seafood available each day. The kitchen utilizes a brick oven, smokehouse, orchard and herb/vegetable garden to create unique California cuisine. Carefully selected premium imported and domestic wines are cellared to complement the varied menu.

This elegant country inn and restaurant is housed in a Victorian mansion built in 1881, but exquisitely renovated by the Muir family eight years ago. Built as a summer home for a wealthy San Franciscan, Madrona Manor is a four-building estate overlooking Dry Creek Valley. Eight beautifully landscaped and wooded acres surround the Manor.

Madrona Manor

Chef Todd Muir's Menu for Eight

Pumpkin Soup with Blue Cheese Cream & Chives
Baby Lettuce Salad
with Baked Goat Cheese Herb Dressing
Grilled Lamb with Cabernet Wine Sauce

Pumpkin Soup with Blue Cheese Cream & Chives

Serves 8
Preparation Time: 45 Minutes

2 cups pumpkin, fresh or canned
1 yellow onion, sliced
2 Tbsps. butter
3 cups chicken stock
    Salt and pepper to taste
    Nutmeg to taste
    Sugar to taste, optional
    Blue cheese, garnish
    Chives, garnish

If using fresh pumpkin, cut pumpkin in half width-wise and remove seeds. Place on a cookie sheet cut side down and bake at 325° for 30 minutes or until soft. Cool and spoon out pumpkin meat.

In a 2 qt. pot, sauté onions in butter until soft and lightly browned. Add pumpkin and chicken stock to the onion and bring to a boil, stirring constantly for 5 minutes.

Purée in a blender until smooth. Adjust seasonings by adding stock if needed. Season to taste with salt, pepper, nutmeg and sugar.

Serve warm, garnished with blue cheese and chives.

Baby Lettuce Salad with Baked Goat Cheese Herb Dressing

Serves 8
Preparation Time: 20 Minutes
Pre-heat oven to 350°

- 1 lb. goat cheese
- 1 cup bread crumbs
- 1 cup olive oil
- ¼ cup balsamic vinegar
- ½ Tbsp. marjoram, chopped
- ½ Tbsp. sage, chopped
- ½ Tbsp. thyme, chopped
- ½ Tbsp. rosemary, chopped
- 8 cups baby lettuce, mixed variety
- 1 red pepper, roasted, julienned
- 1 yellow pepper, roasted, julienned
- Croutons

Roll the goat cheese in bread crumbs. Bake for 10 minutes in 350° oven.

Meanwhile, prepare the herb dressing by combining the olive oil, balsamic vinegar and herbs.

Toss lettuce with the herb dressing. Place the warm goat cheese on top of the lettuce. Garnish with strips of red and yellow peppers and croutons.

Grilled Lamb
with Cabernet Wine Sauce

Serves 8
Preparation Time: 20 Minutes (note marinating time)

1 **lamb leg, boned, about 8 lbs.**
2 **cups olive oil**
1 **cup red wine**
1 **Tbsp. rosemary**
1 **tsp. thyme**
2 **Tbsps. garlic, minced**
2 **Tbsps. shallots, minced**
1 **Tbsp. butter**
½ **bottle cabernet**
2 **cups demi-glace**

Prepare a marinade by combining the olive oil, red wine, rosemary, thyme and garlic. Rub into the lamb leg and marinate for 30 minutes unrefrigerated or overnight in the refrigerator.

Prepare the cabernet sauce by sautéing the shallots in butter. Add the cabernet and demi-glace.

Either grill the marinated lamb or roast it at 375° for 15 minutes or until done. Let rest for 5 minutes before serving.

Serve with warm cabernet wine sauce.

MIXX FOOD, WINE & DRINK

AMERICAN CUISINE
135 Fourth Street
Santa Rosa
573-1344
Lunch Monday–Saturday 11:30AM–2PM
Dinner Monday–Saturday 5:30PM–10PM
AVERAGE DINNER FOR TWO: $40

AN ARRAY OF contemporary American cuisine in a comfortable Art Deco setting best describes Mixx, one of Santa Rosa's most talked about dining establishments.

Creatively using fresh local ingredients, from soup stocks to desserts, menu items are prepared in-house daily. The menu includes fresh seafood, pasta, lamb, beef, poultry, soups and salad which can be ordered as small or large dishes. As a complement to the menu, the award-winning wine list offers an extensive selection.

Mixx is a non-smoking restaurant which offers a full bar, a comfortable atmosphere with a friendly, knowledgeable staff.

Chef Dan Berman's Menu for Four

Ricotta Cheese & Figs in Grape Leaves
Smoked Chicken Fettucine with Sun-dried Tomatoes
Roast Filet with Cabernet Sauvignon
Macadamia Nut Torte

Ricotta Cheese & Figs in Grape Leaves

Serves 4
Preparation Time: 25 Minutes
Pre-heat oven to 350°

¼ **lb. figs, fresh or dried**
½ **cup cream**
 1 **egg**
½ **lb. ricotta cheese**
 4 **Tbsps. pine nuts, toasted**
 2 **Tbsps. chives, chopped**
   Grape leaves

In a food processor, purée figs with cream. Remove and place in mixing bowl. Whisk in egg and ricotta cheese. Fold in pine nuts and chives.

Wrap a teaspoon of filling in individual grape leaves. Place on a sheet pan or cookie pan with parchment paper in 350° oven and bake until warm, about 15 minutes.

Allow to cool slightly before serving.

Cooking tip: Fresh grape leaves may be used but they need to be boiled for 1½ hours in salt water and marinated in olive oil prior to using.

Smoked Chicken Fettucine with Sun-dried Tomatoes

Serves 4
Preparation Time: 25 Minutes

¼ lb. butter, unsalted
5 garlic, cloves, minced
1½ cups sun-dried tomato halves
½ lb. smoked chicken, diced large
2 cups Niçoise olives, pitted
1 cup white wine
1 cup chicken stock
1½ cups cream
   Salt and pepper to taste
1 lb. fresh fettucine

Heat butter in skillet and add garlic, tomatoes, smoked chicken and olives. Stir about 2 minutes and add wine, stirring constantly. Reduce sauce by half and add chicken stock, bringing the mixture to a boil. Reduce by half and add cream, bringing sauce to a boil. When sauce has thickened, remove from heat and season with salt and fresh cracked black pepper.

Cook fresh pasta in boiling water 2 to 3 minutes. Drain pasta and toss with sauce.

Serve on a warm plate.

Cooking tip: This dish complements fresh basil and garlic fettucine.

Roast Filet with Cabernet Sauvignon

Serves 4
Preparation Time: 45 Minutes
Pre-heat oven to 375°

> **Cooking oil**
1½ **lb. filet**
1 **carrot, peeled, chopped**
2 **celery stalks, chopped**
1 **yellow onion, chopped**
1 **Tbsp. butter, unsalted**
2 **Tbsps. shallots, diced**
1 **Tbsp. truffle pieces**
4 **Tbsps. cassis**
1 **bottle cabernet sauvignon**
2 **cups veal stock**
2 **Tbsps. basil, chopped fine**

Take a large roasting pan and add enough oil to cover bottom. Heat until hot and brown filet on each side. Remove pan from heat and place carrots, celery and onion inside roasting pan. Top with filet and bake at 375° for 15–20 minutes or until done. Remove filet from oven and allow to rest for 10 minutes. Slice 2 equal pieces of filet per plate.

Prepare the sauce by melting the butter in a large sauté pan. Add the shallots and cook until soft. Add the truffles and cassis and bring to a boil. Add the cabernet sauvignon and reduce sauce by ⅔. Add the veal stock and reduce by half. Season with salt and fresh ground black pepper.

To serve, ladle sauce on individual plates. Place filet and vegetables on top of sauce and garnish with basil.

Macadamia Nut Torte

Serves 4
Preparation Time: One Hour
Pre-heat oven to 350°

    Parchment paper
    Melted butter
  1 **cup macadamia nuts**
  ¾ **cup sugar**
  2 **Tbsps. flour**
  1 **cup semi-sweet chocolate, grated**
  8 **extra large eggs, separated**
  1 **tsp. macadamia nut liqueur**

Prepare a 10″ cake pan by lining the bottom with a circle of parchment paper and coating the sides and bottom of pan with melted butter.

Grind nuts, ½ cup sugar and the flour in a food processor until the nuts are ground fine.

In a large bowl, combine the nut mixture and grated chocolate. Add egg yolks and macadamia nut liqueur. Set aside.

Whip egg whites until foamy, then add the remaining ¼ cup sugar slowly. Whip to a firm peak. Slowly fold in the egg whites into the chocolate mixture until combined.

Bake immediately at 350° for about 40 minutes or until center of torte springs back when touched. Cool. Serve with broiled coconut topping. (Recipe follows.)

Cooking tip: We suggest using "Altesse," a French semi-sweet chocolate if possible.

Broiled Coconut Topping

Preparation Time: 10 Minutes

½ **cup butter**
1 **cup brown sugar**
¼ **cup milk**
¼ **cup macadamia nuts, chopped**
½ **cup shredded coconut**

Cream butter and brown sugar. Add milk, nuts and coconut. Spread topping over the 10″ macadamia nut torte, using a fork. Broil torte until topping is bubbly and slightly golden.

RESTAURANT MATISSE

FRENCH & AMERICAN CUISINE
620 Fifth Street
Santa Rosa
527-9797
Lunch, Monday–Friday 11:30AM–2PM
Dinner, Monday–Saturday 6PM–9PM
AVERAGE DINNER FOR TWO: $40

LOCATED IN DOWNTOWN Santa Rosa, Restaurant Matisse offers an ever-changing variety of New French and New American specialties. The intimate dining room is graced by fresh flowers, sparkling mirrors and striking prints by Matisse.

Michael Hirschberg, owner and chef, writes a new menu each day to include specialities of grilled fish, local poultry and meats, innovated pâtés, salads and home-baked goodies. House specialties include pork tenderloin with a wild blackberry sauce, breast of chicken stuffed with pear and ham mousse, braised Sonoma rabbit with Andouille sausage with rock shrimp and grilled Petaluma duck in a fresh rhubarb sauce.

Restaurant Matisse takes great pride in its award-winning wine list, which boasts over 180 carefully chosen selections, including many of Sonoma County's most prestigious labels. Premium wines are offered by the glass, and a number of ports and late-harvest wines are listed on the dessert menu.

RESTAURANT

matisse

Chef Michael Hirschberg's Menu for Six

Duck Liver Pâté
Grilled Swordfish with Lemon & Oregano
Baked Vanilla Creams with Caramel Kahlua Sauce

Duck Liver Pâté

Serves 6
Preparation Time: One hour (note refrigeration time)
Pre-heat oven to 350°

¾ lbs. fresh duck livers
1 cup heavy cream
5 egg yolks
1 tsp. salt
1 tsp. white pepper
¾ tsp. allspice
1 cup butter, melted
4 Tbsps. brandy
Parchment paper

Purée livers and force through a fine sieve. Blend in cream, egg yolks, salt, pepper and allspice. Slowly mix in melted butter and brandy.

Pour liver mixture into a mold lined with buttered parchment paper. Place mold into a large pan filled with water (bain-marie) and bake at 350° for 45 minutes. Test for doneness with a toothpick or thermometer reading of 125.°

Chill well before serving.

Grilled Swordfish
with Lemon & Oregano

Serves 6
Preparation Time: 25 Minutes (note marinating time)

 2 lbs. fresh swordfish or tuna
¾ cup virgin olive oil
 4 Tbsps. fresh oregano, chopped
   Zest from 1 lemon
   Black pepper
 3 Tbsps. lemon juice
 1 Tbsp. capers

Skin, trim and slice swordfish or tuna into six steaks.

Combine ¼ cup olive oil, 2 Tbsps. oregano, zest from 1 lemon and black pepper to make marinade. Rub the marinade over the fish filets and marinate for 30 minutes to 4 hours.

Whisk the remaining ½ cup olive oil with the lemon juice, forming a light emulsion. Stir in 2 Tbsps. oregano and capers. Set sauce aside.

Remove fish from marinade and cook over grill or in heavy iron skillet. Use high heat so the fish cooks quickly without drying.

Spoon sauce over steaks. Serve immediately.

Cooking tip: Red potatoes and broccoli make good accompaniments.

Baked Vanilla Creams

Serves 6
Preparation Time: 1½ Hours (note refrigeration time)
Pre-heat oven to 300°

    3 cups cream
    1 vanilla bean
      Pinch of salt
    6 egg yolks, beaten
    ½ cup sugar

Over medium heat, combine the cream, vanilla bean and salt and bring to a simmer.

In a large mixing bowl, blend the beaten egg yolks and sugar. Pour in the hot cream in a slow stream, whisking constantly to avoid lumps. Do not whisk too vigorously or the mixture will get foamy. Split the vanilla bean and scrape the seeds into the mixture. Strain into a pitcher and skim off any bubbles.

Place ramekins in a baking pan and fill with the vanilla cream. Place pan in oven and carefully pour hot water around ramekins to half their height. Loosely cover with foil and bake until firm around the edges, about 1 hour.

Cool and chill for at least 3 hours before serving. Serve baked vanilla creams on top of the caramel Kahlua sauce.

Caramel Kahlua Sauce

    1¾ cups hot water
     2 cups sugar
     ¼ cup Kahlua
     ¼ cup espresso

Over high heat, combine ½ cup water and sugar until caramelized. Slowly add 1¼ cups hot water and reduce heat to low, stirring until dissolved. Remove from heat and add Kahlua and espresso. Cool before serving with baked vanilla creams.

WINEMAKERS' RECIPES

*The following pages contain
treasured recipes from the
most talented of California's
winery chefs.*

Barbecue Chicken Salad

Serves 4
Preparation Time: 25 Minutes

1 large chicken, sliced for grilling
1 cup barbecue sauce
2 cubes chicken bouillon
¼ cup Korbel Brut champagne
   Juice of 1 orange
4 Tbsps. soy sauce
2 Tbsps. sesame seed oil
1 cup olive oil
1 Tbsp. white wine Worcestershire sauce
1 Tbsp. balsamic vinegar
1 tsp. Cajun seasoning or cayenne pepper
1 tsp. oregano
2 cloves garlic, finely chopped
2 heads butterleaf lettuce
2 shallots, sliced thin
¼ cup Asaggio or Parmesan cheese, grated
¼ cup Brazil nuts or hazelnuts, chopped

Grill the chicken with the barbecue sauce. Chill. Discard bones and excess skin. Cut chicken into chunks. Set aside.

Prepare the dressing in a blender or food processor by dissolving the chicken bouillon in the champagne. Add the orange juice, soy sauce, sesame seed oil, olive oil, Worcestershire, vinegar, Cajun seasoning, oregano and garlic. Process until well mixed.

Assemble the salad in a large bowl with the lettuce, chicken, dressing and shallots, tossing well. Portion on chilled salad plates and garnish with grated cheese and nuts.

Cooking tip: This recipe is perfect for leftover chicken and can be prepared a day in advance and assembled at the last minute.

Cheese Sticks

Serves 6
Preparation Time: 20 Minutes
Pre-heat oven to 350°

1½ **cups flour**
  3 **tsps. baking powder**
  ½ **cup Fontina or Monterey Jack cheese, grated**
  ½ **cup cold unsalted butter**
  1 **large egg**
    Milk
    Parmesan cheese

Mix flour and baking powder in a food processor. Add butter in pieces and pulse on and off until mixture is coarse. Add cheese and mix. Add egg and mix until a ball forms.

Roll out dough ¼″ thick into a 12″ × 17″ rectangle. Cut into cheese sticks of ½″ × 5″ lengths.

Place cheese sticks on an ungreased cookie sheet and lightly brush with milk. Sprinkle with Parmesan cheese.

Bake at 350° for 10 to 15 minutes.

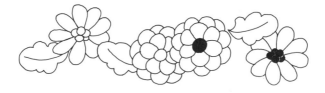

Chèvre Soufflé

Serves 6
Preparation Time: 25 Minutes
Pre-heat oven to 450°

1½ cups milk
  1 cup whipping cream
  6 Tbsps. unsalted butter
  5 Tbsps. all-purpose flour
  ½ tsp. salt
  ¼ tsp. freshly ground black pepper
  ¼ tsp. nutmeg
  5 egg yolks, beaten
  1 cup chèvre
  8 egg whites, beaten
  2 bunches watercress, stems removed
     Vinaigrette
 12 sun-dried tomatoes, sliced thin

In a saucepan, combine the milk and cream over medium heat until scalded. Set aside.

In a separate saucepan, melt the butter and stir in the flour, cooking for 2 minutes. Stir in the hot milk and bring to a boil. Reduce heat and cook until thick, about 5 minutes. Add salt, pepper and nutmeg and remove from heat.

In a large mixing bowl, combine the beaten egg yolks, the warm milk sauce and the chèvre. Slowly add the beaten egg whites.

Spoon into a buttered 12-inch oval platter or a 2-quart soufflé dish. Bake at 450° for 15 minutes or until well browned.

To serve, toss the watercress with the vinaigrette and arrange on individual plates. Top with a serving of the soufflé and surround with slices of sun-dried tomatoes.

Goat Cheese Torta

Serves 8
Preparation Time: 30 Minutes (note refrigeration time)

  1 lb. mild goat cheese or cream cheese
  ½ lb. unsalted butter
  ¾ cup sun-dried tomatoes, packed in oil, drained
  2 cups basil, firmly packed
  4 cloves garlic
  ½ tsp. salt
  ½ tsp. pepper
  ⅓ cup olive oil

In a food processor, combine the goat cheese and butter until well blended. Set aside. In the processor chop the sun-dried tomatoes. Set aside. In the processor chop the basil and garlic together. Season with salt and pepper. With the motor running, slowly drizzle in the oil and process until basil is puréed, then set aside.

Line a 3-cup mold or loaf pan with plastic wrap. Spread ⅓ of the goat cheese mixture in the bottom of the mold. Spread with ½ cup of the basil. Top with another ⅓ of the cheese. Spread with sun-dried tomatoes and top with remaining cheese. Refrigerate until firm, at least 1 hour.

To serve, unmold onto plate and spread on crackers or toasted garlic croutons.

Grilled Leeks with Mustard Cream

Serves 6
Preparation Time: 15 Minutes

6 Tbsps. butter, room temperature
1 Tbsp. Dijon style mustard
¼ cup whipping cream
16 leeks
   Olive oil
   Salt and freshly ground black pepper

Prepare the Mustard Cream by combining the butter, mustard and whipping cream, blending until smooth. Set aside.

Split leeks lengthwise and wash thoroughly. Brush with oil and season with salt and pepper. Grill over a medium-hot mesquite fire until cooked through, turning after about 10 minutes.

Serve hot with Mustard Cream spooned over the top.

Harvest Soup

Serves 6
Preparation Time: 45 Minutes

4 Tbsps. butter
½ onion, minced
2 shallots, minced
1 stalk celery, minced
1 carrot, peeled and minced
2 cups canned pumpkin
2 cups chicken broth
1 cup half and half
½ cup heavy cream
¼ cup Buena Vista Chardonnay
¼ cup orange juice
1 cup sour cream
1 tsp. fresh chives
2 tsps. orange zest, grated
Salt
Hot red pepper sauce

Over medium heat, melt butter in a saucepan and cook the onions, shallots, celery and carrot, stirring constantly until softened, about 7 minutes. Stir in pumpkin and chicken broth. Simmer uncovered for 10 minutes.

Transfer to a blender or food processor and purée until smooth. Return to saucepan adding half and half, cream, Chardonnay and orange juice. Heat to just under boiling. Reduce heat and simmer uncovered for 10 minutes. Season soup to taste with salt and red pepper sauce.

Combine the sour cream, chives and orange zest. To serve, top each soup bowl with a dollop of the sour cream mixture.

Leek & Potato Soup
with Avocado Cream

Serves 6
Preparation Time: 25 Minutes

8 cups chicken stock
4 leek whites, chopped
4 large potatoes, cubed
  Salt and pepper to taste
  Dash of white wine to taste
1 large Haas avocado
1 pt. heavy whipping cream

In a large stock pot, combine the chicken stock, leeks, potatoes, salt, pepper and white wine. Simmer ingredients for 20 minutes or until vegetables are very tender. Purée the soup in a food processor until smooth.

While soup is cooking, prepare the avocado cream garnish by whipping the avocado and cream together until fluffy.

To serve, ladle soup into bowls and garnish with the avocado cream.

Mushroom Strata

Serves 6
Preparation Time: One hour (note refrigeration time)

¼ lb. pancetta, bacon or ham
5 green onions, sliced
1½ lbs. mushrooms, sliced
⅓ cup Vichon Chevrignon
1¼ cups milk
1 loaf day-old French bread
1 cup grated Swiss cheese
5 eggs, beaten
½ cup heavy cream
  Salt and pepper to taste

Slice and cut pancetta into ¼" pieces. Sauté over medium low heat for 10 minutes. Add green onions and sauté briefly. Add mushrooms and sauté until mushrooms are cooked. Remove from heat and season with salt and pepper.

In a shallow dish, mix the wine and milk. Slice bread into ½" pieces and dip into the milk. Place the bread into a buttered 12" round or oval gratin dish. Cover the bread with the mushroom mixture and then sprinkle with the grated cheese. Cover this mixture with another layer of bread dipped into the milk, slightly overlapping the bread slices.

Season the beaten eggs with salt and pepper, and pour evenly over the layers in the dish. Cover and refrigerate overnight.

Remove strata from refrigerator and allow to reach room temperature. Pre-heat oven to 350.° Drizzle top of strata with cream and bake for 45 minutes until puffy and browned.

Pear and Swiss Cheese Salad

Serves 8
Preparation Time: 20 Minutes

12 **Bosc pears, peeled, cored, julienned**
¾ **lb. Swiss cheese, julienned**
¾ **cups walnuts, coarsely chopped**
½ **cup fresh lemon juice**
½ **cup walnut oil**
 1 **cup olive oil**
   Pinch of sugar

Combine pears, cheese and walnuts in a large bowl.

Prepare the dressing by whisking together the lemon juice, walnut oil, olive oil and sugar.

Pour dressing over the salad and mix to coat. Serve immediately.

Cooking note: This is a simple yet elegant salad that is bound to have your guests wanting more. This dish accompanies the Smoked Chicken Fettucine with Basil and Pinenuts on page 165.

Prosciutto Wild Mushroom Bread

Serves 12
Preparation Time: 45 Minutes
Pre-heat oven to 350°

¼ lb. prosciutto, thick slices, diced
¾ cup Kenwood Sauvignon Blanc
1 cup shallots, peeled, chopped
2 cloves garlic, minced
6 Tbsps. butter
2 lbs. mushrooms, sliced (shiitake, chanterelle, oyster)
1 cup Italian parsley, chopped
3 Tbsps. fresh thyme, chopped
  Salt and pepper to taste
1 large loaf sourdough French bread
  Olive oil

In a sauté pan, cook the prosciutto in 2 Tbsps. butter until crisp. Remove the prosciutto and reserve. Deglaze the pan with Sauvignon Blanc and set aside.

In a large pan, sauté the shallots and garlic in 4 Tbsps. butter until transparent. Add the mushrooms, parsley, thyme, salt and pepper. Cook until the mushrooms have released their liquid and the mixture is almost dry. Add the reserved prosciutto and Sauvignon Blanc. Cook over medium heat until the wine is reduced to 2 Tbsps. Set aside to cool.

Slice the bread in half and remove the soft interior, leaving ½-inch thickness of bread on the crust surface. Fill the loaf with the prosciutto, mushroom mixture. Replace the top of the loaf and brush the crust with olive oil. Place on a cookie sheet and bake for 20 minutes.

May be served hot or at room temperature. Slice just before serving.

Spinach Balls with Sauvignon Blanc Mustard Sauce

Makes approximately 35
Allow 3 to 4 per person
Preparation Time: 25 Minutes

One 10 oz. pkg. frozen spinach, chopped (fresh may be used)
1 cup herb stuffing mix, crushed
2 green onions, chopped
2 Tbsps. Parmesan cheese, grated
2 eggs
3 Tbsps. butter
1 shallot, chopped fine
Dash of grated nutmeg
2 Tbsps. dry mustard
2 Tbsps. white wine vinegar
⅓ cup Cakebread Cellars Sauvignon Blanc
1 tsp. sugar
1 egg
3 Tbsps. Dijon mustard
Salt and white pepper to taste

If using frozen spinach, squeeze until dry. Combine the first 8 ingredients and mix well. Shape into 1-inch balls. Cover and refrigerate or freeze until ready to bake.

Bake at 350° for 10 to 12 minutes on an ungreased baking sheet.

In a saucepan, combine the dry mustard, vinegar, Sauvignon Blanc, sugar, egg and Dijon mustard. Cook over low heat, mixing constantly until light, fluffy and thick. Salt and pepper to taste. Add a little more Sauvignon Blanc if too hot or too thick.

To serve, place 3 or 4 spinach balls on top of a dollop of the Mustard Sauce.

Torta Rustica

Serves 10
Preparation Time: 1½ Hours
Pre-heat oven to 375°

4 cups all-purpose flour, unsifted
1 tsp. salt
1 cup butter, cut into pieces
2 whole eggs
2 egg yolks
⅓ cup milk
¼ cup olive oil
2 leeks, sliced thin, white parts only
1 large bulb fennel, chopped coarsely
2 cups frozen spinach, chopped
1 cup Ricotta cheese
¼ cup pesto
Salt and pepper to taste
⅓ cup Parmesan cheese, grated
⅓ cup Mozzarella cheese, grated
¼ lb. salami, sliced thin (optional)
1 red pepper, roasted, skin removed
Egg yolk to brush on top crust

In processor, mix flour and salt. Add butter and mix until mixture is coarse. Blend eggs and milk separately, then add to processor. Mix just until dough forms a ball. Wrap and let rest for 30 minutes in refrigerator.

Sauté leeks and fennel in olive oil until limp. Set aside. Thaw and wring spinach dry. Mix spinach, Ricotta, pesto, salt and pepper and set aside. Mix grated cheeses and set aside. Cut pepper into thin strips.

Roll out ¾ of the dough and place into a 8- or 9-inch spring-form pan, making sure some of the dough overlaps the side of the pan. Layer half the ingredients, starting with the leeks and fennel mixture, spinach mixture, cheese, salami and red pepper; then repeat layers. Roll out remaining dough and place on top of Torta. Crimp edges of dough together, creating a lip. Brush with egg yolk and bake at 375° for 1 hour or until golden.

Cut Torta in wedges to serve, warm or cold.

Warm Goat Cheese Salad
with Golden Pepper Dressing

Serves 8
Preparation Time: 30 Minutes
Pre-heat oven to 400°

1 **log goat cheese cut into 8 rounds**
1 **egg, beaten**
  Breadcrumbs
1 **yellow bell pepper, roasted, peeled, seeded**
2 **Tbsps. rice vinegar**
1 **Tbsp. lemon juice**
  Tabasco to taste
¼ **cup avocado oil**
2 **tbsps. Sauvignon Blanc**
8 **cups fresh lettuce greens**
4 **sun-dried tomatoes, diced (optional)**

Dip cheese rounds into egg and roll in breadcrumbs. Bake on cookie sheet at 400° for 10 minutes.

Prepare the dressing by combining the bell pepper, vinegar, lemon juice and Tabasco in a blender. Process until puréed. Add oil a little at a time and thin, if necessary, with Sauvignon Blanc.

Place fresh lettuce greens on individual salad plates. Put warm cheese rounds on top of lettuce. Drizzle dressing over cheese and sprinkle with sun-dried tomatoes.

Wild Rice Salad

Serves 6
Preparation Time: 25 Minutes

6 cups cooked wild rice, preferably cooked in chicken stock
6 scallions, sliced thin
½ cup skinless almonds, chopped
1 head radicchio, chopped
2 ears of corn, blanched, kernels sliced off cob
2 Tbsps. fresh dill, chopped
   Salt and pepper to taste
2 tsps. Dijon mustard
2 tsps. Balsamic vinegar
½ cup hazelnut oil
½ cup corn oil

Combine the rice, scallions, almonds, radicchio, corn and dill. Season with salt and pepper. Set aside.

Prepare the vinaigrette by blending the mustard, vinegar, hazelnut oil and corn oil. Season with salt and pepper. Pour vinaigrette over salad before serving.

Cooking tip: The beauty of this salad is its versatility with many wines. With its hazelnut oil vinaigrette, it will go nicely with a Chardonnay. Because of the dill, it will also show well with a Sauvignon Blanc. Grilled chicken, shrimp, white meat dishes are fine accompaniments. To serve the salad with red meats such as lamb or beef in order to pair it with a Cabernet Sauvignon, merely use walnut oil instead of hazelnut and replace the almonds with toasted walnuts or pecans. And change the herb to tarragon.

Smoked Chicken Fettucine with Basil & Pinenuts

Serves 4
Preparation Time: 20 Minutes

  1 **clove garlic, minced**
  1 **cup smoked chicken, diced**
 ½ **cup butter**
  1 **bunch fresh basil, chopped**
  1 **tomato, peeled, seeded, chopped**
  1 **lb. fettucine, cooked al dente**
  2 **cups heavy cream**
 ¼ **cup Parmesan cheese, grated**
 ¼ **cup pinenuts, toasted**
     Salt and white pepper to taste

Sauté garlic and chicken in ¼ cup butter. Add basil and tomato and sauté briefly. Add heavy cream, cooking over high heat to reduce by half, about 2 minutes. Add remaining butter and remove from heat.

Combine sauce with cooked fettucine. Stir in Parmesan cheese and season to taste with salt and pepper.

Sprinkle each portion with pinenuts. Garnish with a basil sprig.

Pasta with Shrimp, Asparagus and Cream Sauce

Serves 6
Preparation Time: 40 Minutes

     4 Tbsps. butter
     1 lb. medium shrimp
     1 lb. asparagus
     4 Tbsps. olive oil
     3 cloves garlic, crushed
     1 cup Chalk Hill Winery Sauvignon Blanc
  1 ½ cups whipping cream
     3 Tbsps. arrowroot
        Salt and white pepper
     1 lb. pasta
   ½ bunch cilantro, chopped

In 2 Tbsps. butter, sauté the shrimp. Add asparagus and steam about 2 minutes. Set aside.

Heat remaining butter and 2 Tbsps. oil in a large saucepan and sauté the garlic. Add the wine and reduce by half. Add the cream and arrowroot, whisking together until sauce is thick. Season with salt and pepper.

Cook pasta in boiling water with salt and 2 Tbsps. olive oil.

In a large bowl, toss drained pasta with the shrimp and asparagus and the sauce. Sprinkle with cilantro and serve.

Pasta with Shrimp
in Lemon Butter Sauce

Serves 4
Preparation Time: 45 Minutes

- 1 **cup fresh or frozen baby lima beans**
- 1 **lemon**
- 2 **sprigs fresh thyme or large pinch dried**
  Salt and pepper
- 2 **cups bowtie pasta**
- ½ **cup dry white wine**
- 1 **shallot, diced**
- ¼ **lb. soft butter, cut into chunks**
- 20 **medium shrimp, peeled, deveined, butterflied**
- ¼ **bunch parsley, chopped**

Place the beans in small saucepan and cover with cold water. Add the zest of half the lemon, thyme, salt and pepper to taste. Bring beans to a boil and gently simmer uncovered for 20 minutes if beans are fresh or 15 minutes if frozen. Beans should be firm enough to keep their shape but still tender. Drain and keep warm.

Cook pasta in boiling water, drain. Set aside.

In a saucepan, reduce the wine, juice of the lemon, shallot and remaining lemon zest by half. Gradually whisk in butter. Strain and keep warm.

Sauté shrimp in olive oil for 2 minutes on each side.

To serve, arrange pasta and beans in warm soup bowls. Top with shrimp and drizzle with sauce. Garnish with parsley.

Risotto with Smoked Chicken, Caramelized Onions and Walnuts

Serves 4
Preparation Time: 45 Minutes

12 **Tbsps. butter**
 1 **cup arborio rice**
1½ **qts. chicken stock**
 1 **medium onion, sliced**
 2 **cups smoked chicken, diced**
 ½ **cup walnuts, chopped**
 2 **cups dry jack or Parmesan cheese, grated**
   Salt and pepper to taste

In a medium-sized saucepan, melt 4 Tbsps. butter. Add the arborio rice and stir until hot. Slowly add the chicken stock, stirring constantly. Keep adding stock when the previous amount is cooked into the rice. This a long process that requires constant attention, 30 to 45 minutes, but you will reap the rewards.

At the same time you are cooking the rice you can also caramelize the onions. Melt the remaining 8 Tbsps. butter in a separate saucepan and cook the onions slowly over medium heat until golden brown. Drain and set aside.

When the risotto has absorbed all of the stock, add the chicken, walnuts, caramelized onions and cheese. Stir constantly until cheese has melted and the risotto takes on a creamy look. Season with salt and pepper, serve immediately.

Spaghettini Primavera

Serves 4
Preparation Time: 45 Minutes

1 lb. hot Italian sausage
4 Tbsps. olive oil
2 cloves garlic, minced
   One 28 oz. can Italian plum tomatoes, drained, chopped
1 cup parsley, chopped
1 sprig of fresh oregano or 1 tsp. dried
   Salt and black pepper to taste
1 lb. dried Italian spaghetti
½ lb. zucchini, sliced thin
3 red bell peppers, sliced
½ lb. Chinese snow pea pods
¼ cup fresh basil, chopped
¾ cup Parmesan cheese, grated

Cover sausages in water and boil until cooked, about 30 minutes. When cooked, peel and slice thin.

Heat 2 Tbsps. oil in a heavy skillet over medium heat. Add the cooked sausage and brown. Remove sausage and discard all but 2 Tbsps. fat from skillet. Add the garlic and sauté until transparent, do not brown. Add tomatoes, parsley, oregano, salt and pepper. Cover and simmer for 15 minutes. Add a little water if sauce is too dry. Add the sausage, cover and keep warm.

Cook the spaghetti according to directions while you complete the sauce.

In a skillet, add the remaining 2 Tbsps. oil and heat to medium-high. Quickly sauté the zucchini, red bell peppers and snow peas until snow peas turn a bright green.

Add the vegetables to the sauce and toss thoroughly with the pasta and basil. Sprinkle with parsley and Parmesan cheese.

Roasted Turkey with Herbed Pasta

Serves 4
Preparation Time: 10 Minutes

   3 **cups heavy cream**
   3 **cubes chicken bouillon**
   1 **lb. roasted turkey breast, skinned, shredded**
   1 **lb. herbed pasta**
½ **cup pinenuts, toasted**
   1 **cup Parmesan cheese, grated**

In a large skillet, over medium heat, combine the cream and bouillon cubes, stirring often. When cream becomes slightly thick and lightly coats the back of a wooden spoon, add the turkey and reduce heat.

Cook pasta until tender, drain and rinse under hot water.

Ladle a small amount of the cream sauce, onto warmed plates. Add pasta and ladle more sauce with turkey on top of the pasta. Sprinkle with pinenuts and cheese.

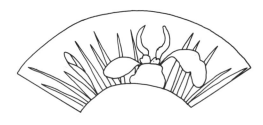

Barbecued Leg of Lamb

Serves 8
Preparation Time: 30 Minutes (note marinating time)

   Leg of lamb
 1 **cup olive oil**
   Juice of one large lemon
   Half bunch parsley, chopped
 3 **Tbsps. rosemary, crushed**
 6 **garlic cloves, crushed**
   Black pepper to taste
 1½ **cups St. Francis Merlot**

Remove the bone from the lamb and slightly butterfly, just to open. Remove all the fat.

Prepare the marinade by combining the olive oil, lemon juice, parsley, rosemary, garlic and black pepper.

Place the lamb and marinade in a large zip-lock bag and refrigerate for at least 24 hours. An hour before barbecuing, add the Merlot.

Skewer the lamb crosswise to hold flat. Cook over hot coals until medium, about 20 minutes, basting frequently.

Cut crossgrain into serving slices. Enjoy!

Grilled Rack of Lamb with Cabernet Lamb Sauce

Serves 8
Preparation Time: 45 Minutes (note marinating time)

  1 **cup pomegranate juice**
  1 **cup Cabernet Sauvignon**
¼ **cup olive oil**
  2 **Tbsps. fresh rosemary**
  2 **Tbsps. fresh thyme**
  2 **Tbsps. shallots, chopped**
  6 **cloves garlic, chopped**
  1 **tsp. black peppercorns**
  3 **racks of lamb, 8 ribs per side**
½ **cup parsley, chopped fine**
½ **cup basil, chopped fine**
      Dijon mustard

Combine the pomegranate juice, Cabernet, olive oil, rosemary, thyme, shallots, 4 cloves of chopped garlic and the peppercorns and rub into the lamb that has been trimmed of fat. Let marinate for 2 to 3 hours.

In a small bowl, combine the parsley, basil and 2 cloves of garlic. Set aside.

Place racks of lamb on the barbecue, searing briefly on each side. Cover barbecue with a lid and cook, turning every 5 minutes. After about 15 minutes, put on a thin layer of mustard and pat on a coating of the herb mixture. Total cooking time will be 20 to 30 minutes.

Cabernet Lamb Sauce

Make a rich lamb stock with well browned bones. Add 2 cups Cabernet Sauvignon, 2 Tbsps. lamb marinade and reduce until desired consistency. Adjust seasonings. Add 1 tsp. of butter to bind the sauce together. Spoon over end of chops on plate.

Lamb with Oyster Mushroom Ragout

Serves 6
Preparation Time: 15 Minutes for sauce

Leg of lamb
¼ **lb. butter, melted**
10 **cloves garlic, minced**
 2 **red onions, thinly sliced**
 6 **cups oyster mushrooms, chopped**
 4 **bouillon cubes added to ½ cup water**
 1 **cup Hop Kiln Johannisberg Riesling**
 1 **tsp. rosemary, chopped**
 1 **tsp. thyme, chopped**
   Salt and pepper to taste

Grill or bake the leg of lamb as desired.

Sauté above ingredients over low heat until mixture thickens, stirring constantly. If ragout fails to thicken, add mixture of 1 Tbsp. cornstarch dissolved in ⅛ cup Riesling and stir constantly until gravy-like consistency.

Remove from heat and serve over sliced leg of lamb.

Merlot Meat Loaf

Serves 6
Preparation Time: 1 Hour
Pre-heat oven to 350°

 1 **cup large breadcrumbs**
¾ **cup Merlot**
 2 **lbs. ground chuck**
 1 **lb. ground pork shoulder**
 1 **large onion, chopped fine**
 4 **cloves garlic, minced**
 1 **cup stuffed green olives, chopped**
½ **cup tomato paste**
 2 **tsps. mustard**
 2 **tsps. basil, chopped**
 2 **tsps. parsley, chopped**
 3 **eggs, beaten**
    Salt and pepper to taste

Combine the breadcrumbs and red wine in a small bowl. Set aside.

Thoroughly combine all the ingredients, except the eggs and soaking breadcrumbs, in a mixing bowl. Then add the beaten eggs and soaked breadcrumbs to the meat mixture.

Form into a 4-inch thick loaf, and place in the center of a good-sized roasting pan, so the meat is not touching the side.

Bake in a 350° oven for 1½ hours, basting several times with the pan juices and additional red wine, to form a crispy crust. Serve hot or room temperature.

Barbecue Pork Tenderloin

Serves 4
Preparation Time: 25 Minutes (note marinating time)

4 pork tenderloins
½ cup soy sauce
½ cup balsamic vinegar
½ cup olive oil
2 cups red wine
2 Tbsps. cumin
2 Tbsps. crushed chile peppers

Prepare the marinade by mixing together the soy sauce, vinegar, olive oil, red wine, cumin and chile peppers. Add pork tenderloin and marinate for at least 24 hours and up to 72 hours.

Barbecue over medium hot fire for approximately 8 to 10 minutes on each side. Do not overcook. The pork should be pink inside.

Slice and serve.

Grilled Pork Loin

Serves 6
Preparation Time: 1 Hour (note marinating time)

 4 lb. pork loin, boned, tied
¼ cup sugar
 2 Tbsps. salt
 8 coriander seeds
 8 black peppercorns
 8 juniper berries, crushed
 1 tsp. dried thyme
 4 qts. water

In a large crock or pan, combine the sugar, salt, coriander seeds, peppercorns, juniper berries, thyme and water. Immerse pork loin in this brine and cover with a lid. Refrigerate for 24 to 48 hours.

Remove meat from brine and pat dry. Insert a meat thermometer in the thickest portion of the loin and grill loin over a medium-hot mesquite fire, turning until thermometer registers about 160,° about 1 hour.

Pork Chops and Apples

Serves 6
Preparation Time: 1 Hour 45 Minutes
Pre-heat oven to 350°

  6 pork chops
  2 Tbsps. oil
  3 large Pippin, Golden Delicious or Macintosh apples
¼ cup brown sugar
½ tsp. cinnamon
  2 Tbsps. butter
     Salt and pepper
½ cup sherry

Brown chops in skillet on both sides in oil. Remove and set aside.

Core and slice unpeeled apples ¼-inch thick. Butter a casserole dish and arrange the apple slices to cover. Sprinkle apples with brown sugar and cinnamon. Dot with butter and top with browned pork chops. Drizzle the oil used to cook the chops from the skillet over the top. Season with salt and pepper. Pour sherry over the top, cover and bake at 350° for 1½ hours.

Mustard-Pepper Steak

Serves 4
Preparation Time: 30 Minutes

1½ lbs. boneless beef tenderloin
 3 tsps. black pepper
1½ tsps. olive oil
 ¼ cup brandy
 2 Tbsps. beef broth
 3 Tbsps. stoneground mustard
 2 Tbsps. William Wheeler Cabernet Sauvignon
 ½ cup Gorgonzola or blue cheese
 ½ tsp. dry tarragon

Trim fat from tenderloin and slice into 1-inch thick slices, two slices per serving. Cover with ¼ to ½ tsp. cracked pepper per slice. More pepper adds heat, don't overdo the pepper unless you like your steak hot.

Heat a 10″ skillet over medium high heat. Add oil to pan. Cook slices of beef until rich brown on bottom, about 3 to 4 minutes, turn over and cook to desired doneness. Remove pan from heat, transfer meat to a plate, and set in a warm oven to hold.

Add brandy to the skillet and scrape up the cooked bits of beef. Return pan to heat, add the beef broth, mustard and Cabernet and reduce liquid by half, stirring to blend. Add the cheese and tarragon and stir until nearly blended. Leave a little bit of chunkiness to the cheese. Remove from heat.

Place tenderloin on individual serving plates and cover with sauce.

Cooking tip: To give the dish added color and flavor, use a mix of pepper such as cracked red and green peppercorns with black pepper.

Mushroom Veal Stew

Serves 6
Preparation Time: 2 Hours
Pre-heat oven to 350°

⅛ cup Porcini mushrooms
 1 cup water
 1 cup all-purpose flour
 1 Tbsp. salt
 1 tsp. pepper
 1 tsp. cumin
 1 bay leaf, crumbled
¼ cup olive oil
 3 lbs. lean veal stew meat
 6 garlic cloves
 1 onion, chopped
¾ lb. fresh mushrooms
 2 cups Chalk Hill Cabernet Sauvignon
 1 cup beef broth
½ cup parsley, chopped
12 boiling onions

Combine Porcini mushrooms and water in sauce pan and bring to a boil. Set aside

Combine flour, salt, pepper, cumin and bay leaf and dredge meat in mixture. Brown veal in olive oil in a heavy-bottomed pan.

Remove veal and sauté onions, garlic, fresh mushrooms and reserved Porcini mushrooms. Add the Cabernet, beef broth, parsley, boiling onions and browned veal.

Bake in 350° oven for 1½ hours.

Veal Medallions on a Bed of Spinach with Cabernet Sauvignon Sauce

Serves 4
Preparation Time: 45 Minutes (note refrigeration time)

2 lbs. veal loin, boned, trimmed and tied
3 garlic cloves, chopped fine
½ cup mixture of rosemary, thyme, parsley, chopped
1 Tbsp. Porcini mushroom powder, optional
2 Tbsps. olive oil
2 Tbsps. raspberry mustard
   Fresh ground black pepper
3 cups veal demiglace
2 cups Cabernet Sauvignon
1 Tbsp. Porcini mushrooms, dried, crumbled
1 cube unsalted butter
½ cup half and half
2 bunches fresh spinach, stems removed, cleaned

Mix garlic, herbs (reserve 1 Tbsp.), Porcini powder, olive oil and raspberry mustard. Rub paste evenly over veal loin. Sprinkle with pepper. Refrigerate overnight.

Sauté veal in a little olive oil and butter. Sear well on all sides. Place browned veal in roasting pan and bake at 350° for 20 to 30 minutes, until meat thermometer measures 160° (rare) to 170° (medium).

Combine 2½ cups demiglace, wine and dried mushrooms to the skillet that was used to sauté the veal. Bring to a boil and reduce liquid to a thick glaze. Whip in the cube of butter one piece at a time. Add half and half and 1 Tbsp. of reserved mixed herbs to finish. Keep warm.

Sauté spinach with a little butter and the reserved ½ cup of demiglace. Season with salt and pepper.

Let veal rest before slicing. Arrange slices over a bed of spinach. Gently pour sauce over veal and serve immediately.

Cooking tip: The recommended wine is Ferrari-Carano 1986 Alexander Valley Cabernet Sauvignon. Bon Appetito!

Chicken with Chardonnay & Caper Cream

Serves 6
Preparation Time: 20 Minutes

¼ **cup unsalted butter**
 4 **medium shallots, finely chopped**
 1 **lb. chicken breasts**
¼ **cup lemon juice**
¼ **cup De Loach Chardonnay**
 2 **cups heavy cream**
¼ **cup capers, drained**
 2 **lbs. cooked pasta, fettucine or tagliatelli**
¼ **cup parsley, chopped**

In a large skillet, melt the butter over moderate heat. Add the shallots and sauté for 1 minute.

Bone and skin the chicken breasts and cut into ½″ wide strips. Add the chicken pieces to the skillet and increase the heat. Sauté the chicken until lightly browned, 3 to 5 minutes.

Add the lemon juice and Chardonnay, stirring and scraping the bottom of the pan with a wooden spoon to remove any lumps or browned bits. When most of the Chardonnay has evaporated, add the cream. Gently boil until thick, 10 to 12 minutes.

Stir in the capers and serve immediately over pasta. Garnish with chopped parsley.

Cooking tip: Serve with De Loach 1989 Russian River Valley Chardonnay.

Chicken Florentine

Serves 6; Preparation Time: 1½ Hours; Pre-heat oven to 350°

6 chicken breast halves
1 cup seasoned bread crumbs
2 Tbsps. olive oil
2 Tbsps. butter
2 cups Marinara Sauce
   (see following recipe)
½ cup dry red wine
1½ cups chicken stock, boiling
1 cup uncooked long grain rice
1 small can sliced black olives,
   drained

2 10 oz. pkgs.
   chopped spinach,
   thawed, pressed dry
1 cup cottage cheese
2 eggs, beaten
½ tsp. marjoram
½ tsp. salt
½ tsp. nutmeg
⅓ cup Parmesan cheese,
   grated

Coat chicken with bread crumbs. Heat oil and butter in large skillet. Add chicken breast and sauté until brown. Remove from pan and set aside.

Combine Marinara sauce and wine. Place 1 cup sauce/wine mixture in skillet. Add boiling chicken stock, rice and olives, stir thoroughly. Place in a lightly oiled 3 qt. casserole or baking pan. Arrange chicken, skin side down, on top of rice mixture. Cover with foil and bake 20 minutes. Turn chicken, recover with foil and bake another 25 minutes. Can be refrigerated at this point.

While chicken is baking, combine spinach, cottage cheese, eggs, marjoram, salt and nutmeg. Spoon spinach mixture around edge of baking dish. Top with remaining marinara/wine sauce. Sprinkle with Parmesan cheese and bake uncovered 10–15 minutes more.

Marinara Sauce

Makes 3 cups

1 Tbsp. olive oil
3 cloves garlic, minced
1 28 oz. can tomato purée
2 tsps. sugar
2 Tbsps. parsley, chopped

1 bay leaf
1 tsp. oregano
1 tsp. basil
Salt and pepper to taste

Heat olive oil in a large saucepan and sauté garlic lightly. Add remaining ingredients and simmer 35–45 minutes. Remove bay leaf before using in recipe.

Chicken Stuffed with Swiss Chard

Serves 6
Preparation Time: 1½ Hours
Pre-heat oven to 350°

   2 medium-sized chickens
   2 cups Swiss chard, stems chopped
   ¼ lb. mushrooms, sliced
   2 Tbsps. olive oil
   1 clove garlic, minced or pressed
   2 tsps. fresh basil, chopped
   1 tsp. parsley, minced
   1 medium-size onion, minced
   ½ cup bread crumbs
   ½ cup dry Ricotta cheese
   2 eggs
     Salt and pepper

Clean and rinse chickens and pat dry. With meat cleaver, break breastbone and ribs, then halve breast down center with poultry scissors, being careful not to cut through the skin. This is done so the chicken will lay flatter.

Sauté the Swiss chard and mushroom in olive oil. Add the garlic, basil, parsley and onion. When vegetables are lightly cooked, remove from heat and add bread crumbs, Ricotta cheese and the eggs. Lightly salt and pepper to taste. Mix mixture well and divide in half.

Gently push the Swiss chard stuffing under the skin of the chicken, beginning at the front and working back. Truss simply, if necessary. Repeat procedure with other half of stuffing mixture with second chicken.

Bake chicken in a 375° oven for 50 minutes or until meat is no longer pink when slashed near the bone. If chicken becomes too brown near end of cooking, decrease temperature to 350.° Cut chicken into quarters and serve.

Cooking tip: Serve chicken with lightly cooked, peeled asparagus spears, sliced tomatoes and Robert Mondavi Chardonnay.

Chicken with Tomatoes & White Wine

Serves 4
Preparation Time: 30 Minutes

4 Chicken breast halves, boneless, skinless
3 Tbsps. butter
2 Tbsps. olive oil
   Salt and pepper to taste
1 Tbsp. rosemary, chopped
2 garlic cloves, crushed
2 Tbsps. shallots, chopped
¾ cup mushrooms, quartered
One 14 oz. can Italian plum tomatoes
½ cup chicken broth
¾ cup Chalk Hill Chardonnay

Heat butter and oil in a large skillet and brown the chicken breasts. Season with salt, pepper and rosemary. Remove chicken from skillet and keep warm.

In remaining oil, sauté garlic and shallots. Add the mushrooms and tomatoes and cook 5 minutes. Add chicken broth and wine, cooking sauce for 10 minutes. When sauce has reduced, return the chicken to the skillet for 3 minutes, to absorb the sauce flavors.

Transfer chicken to warm plates and serve with tomato wine sauce drizzled over the top.

Grilled Tarragon Chicken Skewers

Serves 6
Preparation Time: 30 Minutes (note marinating time)

    1 cup olive or walnut oil
    1 cup Buena Vista Sauvignon Blanc
    1 Tbsp. fresh tarragon
    ¼ cup parsley, minced
    ½ tsp. Worcestershire sauce
    1 clove garlic, minced
    1 small onion, minced
      Salt and pepper to taste
 1½ lbs. chicken breast cut in 1" chunks
    1 red or yellow bell pepper in 1" chunks
    ½ lb. mushrooms
    1 zucchini in ½" slices
    1 basket cherry tomatoes

Prepare the marinade by whisking together the oil, wine, tarragon, parsley, Worcestershire, garlic, onion, salt and pepper. Marinate the chicken, bell peppers, mushrooms and zucchini in a glass bowl for 2 to 3 hours in the refrigerator, turning occasionally.

Skewer chicken chunks and vegetables.

Grill chicken and vegetables 4 to 5 inches over hot coals, turning frequently. Be careful not to overcook, they should take less than 5 minutes each.

Cooking tip: Serve with Buena Vista Sauvignon Blanc.

Thai Grilled Chicken

Serves 8
Preparation Time: 15 Minutes (note marinating time)

16 **boneless chicken thighs**
 8 **stalks lemongrass, chopped**
20 **green onions**
½ **cup Thai fish sauce**
⅔ **cup sugar**
½ **cup raw peanuts**
   Oil
 3 **Tbsps. sugar**
 1 **tsp. salt**

Make the marinade by adding lemongrass (use only bottom ⅓) and 12 chopped green onions to food processor and pulse until blended. Remove to a mixing bowl and add the fish sauce and sugar.

Marinate the chicken thighs at least three hours or as long as overnight in the refrigerator.

Deep-fry the peanuts in oil, cool, and toss in sugar and salt to a pleasant sweet-salty balance similar to honey roasted peanuts. Set aside.

Grill chicken over a hot fire. Garnish with remaining green onion slices and peanuts.

Duck Steaks with Shallots

Serves 6
Preparation Time: One Hour

  6 duck breasts, skinned
    Salt
    Freshly ground pepper
  2 large cloves garlic, chopped fine
¼ cup parsley, chopped fine
  1 cup duck or chicken stock
  3 Tbsps. butter
  6 shallots, chopped fine
⅔ cup Beringer Cabernet Sauvignon
  2 Tbsps. olive oil
  3 Tbsps. heavy cream

Mix a dash each of salt and pepper with 1 minced clove of the garlic and half of the parsley. Sprinkle some of this mixture on both sides of the duck breasts. Set aside at room temperature for 45 minutes.

Meanwhile, put the stock in a small saucepan over medium heat and reduce it to ⅓ cup. Set aside.

Heat the butter in a skillet, add the shallots and cook them on medium heat until they are soft and have lost all their moisture. Add the wine and reduce by half. Remove to a small bowl.

Add the oil to the same skillet, heating until it almost starts smoking. Add the duck and sear the breasts on one side, then turn them over and season the seared side with salt and pepper. Finish cooking until the meat juices come beading on the seared surface of the meat. Salt the second side. Remove the duck to a serving platter.

To the skillet add the stock and reduce until it coats a spoon with a lacquer. Add the shallots in the wine, the cream and any juice having by now escaped out of the meat. Correct the seasoning of the sauce and add the remaining garlic and parsley.

Drizzle the Cabernet pan gravy over the duck and serve.

Duck with Pear in Champagne

Serves 4
Preparation Time: 1½ Hours
Pre-heat oven to 450°

2 **whole ducks**
   Olive oil
2 **onions, chopped**
2 **carrots, chopped**
1 **celery stick, chopped**
3 **tomatoes, chopped**
1 **bay leaf**
1 **tsp. thyme, chopped**
1 **head garlic, chopped**
4 **Tbsps. flour**
1 **cup brandy**
1 **qt. Gloria Ferrer Brut**
4 **pears, peeled, cored**
   Cinnamon stick
   Peel of 1 orange
   Parsley for garnish

Cut the ducks in half. Set aside the necks, giblets and wing tips. Prick the skin, season to taste with salt and pepper and roast for 1 hour at 450.°

Meanwhile, in a stock pot, sauté the necks, giblets and wing tips in olive oil. Add the onion, carrots, celery, tomatoes, bay leaf, thyme and garlic. Add the flour and deglaze with the brandy and 2 cups champagne. Add enough water to cover duck and bring to a boil. Reduce stock to a simmer.

Poach the pears in the remaining champagne with the cinnamon stick and orange peel.

Strain the giblet stock and add to the poached pears. Cut the ducks in half and put them in the stock-champagne sauce and cook for 10 minutes before serving.

Bay Scallops
with Spinach and Pernod

Serves 4
Preparation Time: 30 Minutes

¾ cup clam juice
1 tsp. shallots, minced
1½ cups cream
   Salt and pepper to taste
1 Tbsp. Pernod
   Juice of 1 lemon
3 bunches spinach, chopped
4 Tbsps. butter
1 Tbsp. olive oil
½ tsp. nutmeg
½ lb. bay scallops, abductor muscle removed
   Lemon zest, garnish
   Caviar, optional, garnish

In a saucepan, combine the clam juice with shallots. When the clam juice has reduced by ⅔, add the cream and season with salt and pepper. Reduce the cream by half, then stir in the Pernod and lemon juice. Strain and keep warm.

Heat the spinach in 1 Tbsp. butter and olive oil. Season with salt, pepper and nutmeg. Divide the spinach onto 4 plates and arrange into small nests.

Sauté the scallops in hot butter until lightly browned and cooked through, about 2 minutes. Divide the scallops among the 4 spinach nests and drizzle the sauce over the top. Garnish with lemon zest and caviar. Serve immediately.

Citrus and Apricot Prawns

Serves: 6
Preparation Time: 25 Minutes (note refrigeration time)

12 large prawns
 3 Tbsps. olive oil
 1 Tbsp. ginger, chopped fine
½ cup scallions, chopped
 2 Tbsps. parsley, chopped fine
 1 Tbsp. white wine
 1 Tbsp. chives, chopped
   Juice of 1 lemon
   Juice of half lime
   Juice of half orange
 3 Tbsps. Grand Marnier Liqueur
 2 Tbsps. candied ginger, chopped fine
   Zest the rind of ½ lemon, ½ orange, ½ lime
½ cup dried apricots, cut into thin strips
 1 cup papaya, diced
   Scallions for garnish
   Parsley for garnish

Wash the prawns, removing the shell but leaving the tail on, and devein. Place on a plate and pat dry with a paper towel.

In a saucepan, heat the olive oil and add the fresh ginger, scallions and parsley. Sauté until the scallions are soft and then add the prawns, wine and chives and continue to stir. As the prawns begin to turn pink in color, add the lemon, lime and orange juice along with the Grand Marnier and candied ginger. Let simmer while adding the three citrus rinds. Remove from heat and refrigerate.

To serve, add dried apricots and payaya and toss to mix. Sprinkle with some fresh chopped scallions and parsley for color.

Cooking tip: This recipe can be served warm. If you cannot find fresh papaya, mango or nectarines also work well.

Grilled Prawns with Tequila & Nectarine Cream Sauce

Serves 4
Preparation Time: 20 Minutes

20 prawns, deveined
 1 cup olive oil
 1 tsp. lavender, optional
 1 tsp. chervil, optional
 1 Tbsp. shallots, chopped
 1 Tbsp. butter
 1 nectarine, diced fine
   Juice of 1 lime
 ½ cup tequila
 2 cups heavy cream
 1 tsp. cumin

Clean prawns and marinate in olive oil with lavender and chervil while preparing the nectarine sauce.

Sauté the shallots in butter until limp. Add the nectarines, lime juice and tequila and bring to a simmer. Reduce liquid until nearly dry. Add the cream and reduce by half or until sauce becomes desired consistency. Whisk in the cumin. Set aside.

Remove excess oil from prawns. Grill on skewers and serve with sauce ladled over.

Cooking tip: Serve with Inglenook-Napa Valley Estate Bottled Chardonnay.

Mussels en Croute

Serves 6
Preparation Time: One Hour

  7 **Tbsps. butter**
  2 **Tbsps. shallots, chopped fine**
  ½ **lb. mushrooms, chopped**
1¾ **cup Chimney Rock Chardonnay**
  ¼ **cup beef bouillon**
     Salt and pepper to taste
  2 **lbs. mussels**
  1 **lb. shrimp, shelled, deveined, chopped**
  1 **onion, chopped**
  2 **Tbsps. flour**
  3 **egg yolks**
  ½ **cup heavy cream**
  ½ **lb. frozen puff pastry**

Melt 4 Tbsps. butter in frying pan and add shallots. Stir 1 minute, add mushrooms, stirring for 5 minutes. Add ¼ cup wine and bouillon. Stir until liquid disappears. Season with salt and pepper. Set aside.

Clean mussels and place in shallow pan with onion and ½ cup wine. Cover and cook for 8 minutes. Remove mussels from shells, discarding any unopened mussels. Set aside. Place shells of shrimp into ⅓ of mussel liquid and simmer for 5 minutes. Strain and set aside.

In a saucepan, prepare the sauce by combining 3 Tbsps. butter and flour together until thick. Add ⅓ of the mussel liquid and 1 cup wine into the saucepan. Stir over medium heat until thickened. Beat egg yolks with cream and stir into the hot mixture until smooth and creamy. Add chopped shrimp. Cool.

Roll puff pastry very thin. Cut into even number of 2″ squares. Place a small amount of shrimp mixture and 2 or 3 mussels on half of the squares. Top with pastry, moisten edges with water and press firmly to seal.

Fry in hot oil until brown. Serve with sauce.

Salmon Poached in Champagne & Cream Sauce with Fresh Papaya

Serves 4
Preparation Time: 30 Minutes

2 cups champagne or sparkling wine
2 cups heavy cream
Four 6 oz. salmon filets
1 papaya, peeled, seeded, quartered
2 Tbsps. unsalted butter

Pour champagne or sparkling wine in skillet large enough to hold the salmon filets. Bring to a boil and reduce by half. Add cream and return to boil. Poach salmon in champagne and cream for 5 minutes at a simmer.

Place a papaya quarter, which has been cut into a fan, on top of each filet and continue to cook until the salmon is done, about 3 minutes. The salmon should be firm to the touch but still moist in the center. Remove salmon from pan and keep warm.

Reduce sauce to about 1 cup. Whisk in butter and pour over salmon.

Cooking tip: 1987 Benzinger of Glen Ellen Blanc de Blancs is a good accompaniment for this dish.

Baked Salmon with Garlic, Basil & Tomatoes

Serves 4
Preparation Time: 20 Minutes
Pre-heat oven to 400°

    4 garlic cloves
    1 cup fresh basil leaves
 2½ Tbsps. olive oil
    ¼ cup fresh lemon juice
One 2 lb. salmon filet
       Salt and ground black pepper
    1 cup shallots, chopped
    ¾ cup Sauvignon Blanc
    1 large tomato, sliced thin crosswise

Mince the garlic and basil leaves in a food processor along with ½ Tbsp. olive oil. Add the lemon juice and pulse to combine. Set this mixture aside.

Brush salmon filet with 2 Tbsps. olive oil, sprinkle with salt and pepper. Line a shallow baking dish with foil, enough to very loosely encase fish and turn up edges. Spread a bed of shallots on the bottom of aluminum foil, and place filet on top.

Heat wine in a small saucepan until warm and pour directly onto foil at the bottom of dish. Spread the basil mixture on the filet and arrange tomato slices on top. Fold foil over top of filet to seal in liquid and steam.

Bake in 400° oven for 20 minutes or until fish is firm.

Grilled Salmon
with Orange Saffron Butter

Serves 6
Preparation Time: 15 Minutes

  6 salmon steaks
   Vegetable oil
   Salt and pepper to taste
¼ **tsp. saffron**
 1 **Tbsp. orange juice**
 1 **tsp. orange zest**
 5 **Tbsps. butter**
 2 **tsps. shallots, chopped**

Brush fish with vegetable oil and season with salt and pepper. Set aside.

Prepare the saffron butter by dissolving the saffron in the orange juice. In a food processor or blender purée the orange juice, orange zest, butter, and shallots.

Grill salmon on each side for 4 to 5 minutes. Serve with a dollop of saffron butter.

Cooking tip: The saffron butter may be prepared in advance and stored in the refrigerator for up to a week. Serve with Franciscan Oakville Estate Chardonnay.

Salmon & Sea Bass
in Buerre Blanc Sauce

Serves 6
Preparation Time: 20 Minutes
Pre-heat oven to 450°

1¼ lbs. salmon filet
1¼ lbs. seabass filet
1¼ cups Hacienda Chardonnay
    Salt and pepper to taste
2 Tbsps. shallots, minced
1 Tbsp. heavy cream
1½ cups soft butter
    American sturgeon caviar, garnish
    Baking parchment paper

Cut fish into 4" × ½" strips. Weave alternate fish to form a 4" square. Place woven squares into buttered baking dish. Add ¼ cup wine and season with salt and pepper. Cover fish with buttered baking parchment and seal baking dish with foil. Place in 450° oven 5 to 7 minutes.

Prepare the sauce by reducing 1 cup wine with shallots to 3 Tbsps. Add cream and bring to a boil. Add butter in small pieces, whisking constantly until butter is incorporated into sauce. Season with salt and pepper.

To serve, place fish on Buerre Blanc Sauce and garnish with caviar.

Salmon with Zinfandel Sauce

Serves 4
Preparation Time: 30 Minutes

　1 lb. salmon filet, bones and skin removed
　　Kosher or coarse salt
　　Coarse black pepper
　1 Tbsp. cooking oil
　1 Tbsp. shallots, chopped fine
　¾ cup Sutter Home Red Zinfandel
　1 Tbsp. heavy cream
　¼ lb. sweet butter, room temperature, sliced

Cut salmon filets into ¼-lb. pieces. Place the salmon between lightly oiled plastic wrap sheets and pound with a chef's knife or meat cleaver until salmon is about ¼″ thick. Lightly sprinkle pounded salmon with salt and pepper.

Heat non-stick frying pan to high heat. Add cooking oil and sauté the salmon quickly until light brown. Turn and sear the other side. Remove from pan to heated platter.

Pour off remaining oil from pan and add the shallots and Sutter Home Red Zinfandel. Reduce over medium-high heat to ¼ cup. Add cream and continue reducing until it thickens. Whisk sweet butter into sauce one piece at a time, beating continuously until all butter is incorporated into a smooth sauce. Pour over salmon and serve.

Swordfish with Wild Mushrooms in Parchment

Serves 4
Preparation Time: 40 Minutes
Pre-heat oven to 375°

4 swordfish steaks, ¾" to 1" thick
1 large shallot, sliced paper thin
1 cup wild mushrooms chopped, (shiitakes, chanterelles, morels)
1 Tbsp. parsley, minced fine
4 tsps. lemon juice
¼ cup dry white wine
4 sheets kitchen parchment paper 12" × 12"

Place each swordfish steak on a sheet of parchment paper. Divide shallots, mushrooms and parsley into 4 equal parts and sprinkle over top of steaks. Bring up side and ends of parchment and pour lemon juice and wine equally over each steak. Bring corners of paper together and tie with kitchen string.

Place parchment packages on 2 baking sheets and then into a 375° oven for 15 to 20 minutes, depending on the thickness of the steaks.

Remove from the oven, slit parchment paper with a knife and serve immediately.

Cooking tip: Serve with V. Sattui 1988 Napa Valley Chardonnay.

Tuna with Lavender

Serves 6
Preparation Time: 30 Minutes (note marinating time)

3 lbs. fresh tuna, cut into 1" slices
2 Tbsps. whole black peppercorns
2 Tbsps. Szechuan peppercorns
2 Tbsps. fresh or 4 Tbsps. dried lavender flowers or buds
2 Tbsps. olive oil
6 Tbsps. butter
3 Tbsps. shallots, minced
1 cup chicken stock
1 cup Simi Cabernet Sauvignon

Crush peppercorns with pestle, or process with steel blade in food processor. Mix pepper with lavender and press into both sides of the tuna slices. Cover and let stand at least 30 minutes, or up to 3 hours for maximum pepper flavor.

Sear over high heat in olive oil and 2 Tbsps. butter for 3 to 4 minutes on each side. Check for desired doneness by piercing with the point of a small, sharp knife. Place fish in a warm oven while making the sauce.

Add shallots to sauté pan and cook about one minute. Deglaze the pan with the stock, then add the Cabernet and cook rapidly until reduced by half. Remove pan from heat and stir in remaining butter.

Pour sauce over tuna and serve immediately.

Cooking tip: Dried lavender is available in many health food stores.

Apricot Crown

Serves 10
Preparation Time: One Hour (note refrigeration time)
Pre-heat oven to 425°

   1 **cup dried apricots**
  ½ **cup sugar**
   2 **eggs**
  ¼ **tsp. grated lemon rind**
   1 **tsp. lemon juice**
   2 **lbs. puff pastry**
  ½ **cup almonds, toasted, chopped**

Place apricots in a saucepan with water to cover. Cook over low heat until soft. Drain and purée. Add sugar, 1 egg, lemon rind and lemon juice. Cool.

Divide puff pastry in half. Roll, then cut a circle 10″ in diameter ¼″ thick and place on parchment-lined baking sheet. Roll and cut a circle 11″ in diameter ¼″ thick.

Sprinkle almonds on 10″ pastry and mound apricot filling in center, leave a 1½″ border. Moisten outside edge of base with water. Cover with 11″ circle. Make a scalloped border by pressing the outside edge of dough toward the center with the dull edge of a knife. Chill 1 hour.

Glaze pastry with 1 beaten egg and bake at 425° for 30 minutes. Reduce heat to 375° and bake for 20 minutes or until golden brown.

Serve while still warm with Freemark Abbey's Edelwein Gold.

Fresh Berries with Basil & Mint

Serves 4
Preparation Time: 10 Minutes (note marinating time)

2 cups fresh raspberries
2 cups fresh blueberries
2 cups fresh strawberries
2 cups fresh ollallieberries
1 cup fresh mint, chopped
1 cup fresh basil, chopped
3 cups Hanns Kornell Champagne
   Ice cream or whipped cream, optional

Clean berries and mix with mint and basil. Pour champagne over berries and marinate overnight.

Serve with ice cream or dollop of whipped cream.

Black Currant Tea Ice Cream

Serves 6
Preparation Time: 45 Minutes

2 **cups milk**
½ **cup black currant tea leaves**
8 **egg yolks**
1 **cup granulated sugar**
2 **cups whipping cream**

In a saucepan, scald the milk and remove from the heat. Place tea leaves in a tea ball or tie in cheesecloth and add to saucepan. Let steep 3 to 4 minutes and remove tea.

Beat egg yolks until light and beat in sugar. Pour in hot tea-flavored milk and stir to blend. Turn into the top pan of a double boiler and cook over simmering water, stirring until custard coats a spoon, about 10 minutes. Cool by nesting the pan in a bowl of ice. Stir in cream and refrigerate until well chilled.

Pour custard into an ice-cream freezer and freeze according to manufacturer's instructions.

Spoon ice cream into dessert bowls. It should be slightly soft for best flavor and texture.

Cherry & Chocolate Trifle

Serves 4
Preparation Time: 30 Minutes

1 Tbsp. sugar
1 Tbsp. cornstarch
1 egg
1 cup skim milk
1 tsp. vanilla extract
¾ cup dried cherries
½ bottle Cakebread Cellars Cabernet Sauvignon
¼ lb. angel food cake
3 Tbsps. sherry
¼ lb. bittersweet chocolate squares

To make the custard, mix the sugar and the cornstarch in a small saucepan. Add the egg and milk, mixing well. Heat to boiling over medium heat stirring constantly, until thickened. Remove from the heat and add the vanilla. Cool to room temperature.

Combine cherries with ½ cup Cabernet until soft and plump. Put in food processor until lightly chopped. Set aside.

Arrange slices of angel food cake into a trifle bowl or large wine goblets. Sprinkle with 1 Tbsp. sherry. Pour ⅓ of the custard over the cake. Spoon ⅓ cup of the cherries over the custard. Repeat the process twice. Cover and refrigerate.

Melt chocolate with remaining Cabernet, on stovetop or in microwave, and drizzle over trifle. Serve immediately.

Cooking tip: Serve with Cakebread Cellars traditional Cabernet Sauvignon or Rutherford Reserve.

Chocolate Decadence Cake

Preparation Time: 1½ Hours
Pre-heat oven to 350°

¼ lb. unsweetened
   chocolate squares
½ cup sweet butter
1 cup boiling water
1 tsp. vanilla extract
2 cups sugar
2 eggs, separated

1 tsp. baking soda
½ cup sour cream
2 cups all-purpose flour,
   sifted
1 tsp. baking powder
1½ cups raspberry purée
   or preserves

Grease and flour a 9-inch round spring-form pan.

Pour boiling water over chocolate and butter, let stand until melted. Stir in vanilla and sugar, then whisk in egg yolks, one at a time, blending well after each addition.

Mix baking soda and sour cream and whisk into chocolate mixture. Sift flour and baking powder together and add to batter.

Beat egg whites until stiff, but not dry. Stir a quarter of the egg whites thoroughly into the batter. Scoop remaining egg whites on top of the batter and gently fold together. Pour batter into the prepared pan. Set on middle rack in oven and bake for 60 to 70 minutes. Cool in pan for 10 minutes and remove.

When cake is cool, carefully slice in half lengthwise. Spread raspberry purée on the bottom half, then replace the top half of the cake. Frost with chocolate frosting.

Chocolate Frosting

2 Tbsps. sweet butter
¾ cup semisweet
   chocolate chips
6 Tbsps. heavy cream

1¼ cups sifted
   confectioners sugar
1 tsp. vanilla extract

Place all ingredients in a heavy saucepan over low heat and whisk until smooth. Cool slightly. Add more sugar if necessary to achieve spreading consistency. Spread on cake while frosting is still warm.

Italian Biscotti

Yields: 4 Dozen
Preparation Time: 45 Minutes
Pre-heat oven to 350°

½ **cup butter**
¾ **cup sugar**
 3 **eggs**
½ **tsp. vanilla**
 3 **cups flour**
 3 **Tbsps. baking powder**
½ **tsp. salt**
 2 **Tbsps. grated lemon peel**
 2 **Tbsps. grated orange peel**
 1 **Tbsp. anise seed**
 1 **cup almonds, chopped**

Cream butter and sugar, then add eggs one at a time, beating well after each addition. Add vanilla.

Sift together flour, baking powder and salt. Slowly add to the creamed mixture. Stir in lemon and orange peels, anise seed and almonds, blending well.

Divide dough into 3 parts and shape each part into a long roll about 1½" in diameter. Place rolls onto cookie sheet several inches apart and flatten slightly.

Bake at 350° for 15 minutes. Remove from oven and slice roll crosswise ¾" thick. Lay cut side down on cookie sheet, return to oven and bake an additional 15 minutes.

Cooking tip: This recipe makes a biscotti that is not very sweet, in the traditional manner of Italian baking. For something different, try dunking these biscotti in a glass of Sebastiani Barbera.

Mousse Grand Cru

Serves 8
Preparation Time: 30 Minutes (note refrigeration time)

1¾ cups Grand Cru Gewurztraminer
¾ cup sugar
2 packages unflavored gelatin
1 can lychees
½ cup syrup from lychees
   Juice of 1 lemon
2 cups cream, whipped
   Strawberries for garnish
   Sabayon sauce (recipe follows)

In a saucepan, combine wine and sugar and simmer until sugar is dissolved. Sprinkle gelatin over lychee syrup, let stand to soften. Add wine mixture to gelatin and stir until dissolved.

Purée drained lychees and press through a sieve. Add purée and lemon juice to gelatin-wine mixture. Chill until syrupy.

Gently fold whipped cream into gelatin mixture. Pour into a single 2 qt. mold or individual molds. Chill until firm. To serve, dip molds into hot water for a few minutes. Invert onto serving plates. Garnish with strawberries and spoon sabayon sauce over the top.

Sabayon Sauce

3 egg yolks
⅓ cup sugar
¾ cup Grand Cru Gewurztraminer
½ cup cream, whipped

In a mixing bowl, beat together egg yolks and sugar until mixture forms a ribbon. Place bowl over simmering water, whisk in Gewurztraminer and continue to beat until mixture is nearly tripled in volume. Remove from heat, cool slightly. Fold in whipped cream and chill until ready to serve.

Orange Custard with Strawberries and Muscat Canelli

Serves 6
Preparation Time: 1 Hour (note refrigeration time)
Pre-heat oven to 350°

2 cups milk
 Zest of 2 oranges
2 whole eggs
4 egg yolks
½ cup sugar
1 tsp. vanilla
2 cups strawberries, cut in half
1 bottle Benzinger of Glen Ellen Muscat Canelli

Scald the milk on high heat with the orange zest. Set aside.

In a large mixing bowl, beat the whole eggs and egg yolks together, then slowly add the sugar. Add the milk, stirring constantly. Add the vanilla and blend well. Strain and pour into individual custard cups.

Place the cups in a shallow baking pan filled with boiling water half way up the sides of the cups. Bake at 350° in the center of the oven for 35 minutes or until the custard feels firm when pressed. Remove from water, cool and chill in refrigerator for at least 2 hours.

Meanwhile, pour Muscat into a small saucepan and bring to a boil, reducing to a ¼-cup syrup consistency. Refrigerate. Toss with strawberries 30 minutes before serving.

To serve, unmold custard onto individual plates. Surround with strawberries and drizzle with the syrup.

Cooking tip: Serve with Benzinger of Glen Ellen 1990 Muscat Canelli.

Pears in Port Sauce

Serves 4
Preparation Time: 15 Minutes (note refrigeration time)

 2 cups Zinfandel Port
 4 pears peeled, halved lengthwise
¾ cup semi-sweet chocolate chips
 1 pt. sour cream
   Mint leaves for garnish

In a saucepan, bring port to a boil. Add pears and reduce to a simmer for 10 minutes. Remove from heat and refrigerate for 3 hours.

Place pears flat side down on a plate and pour remaining port sauce over the top. Drizzle with semi-sweet chocolate. Top with a dollop of sour cream and garnish with fresh mint leaves.

Wine Cake with Muscat À Deux

Preparation Time: One Hour
Pre-heat oven to 350°

One package yellow cake mix
One small package French vanilla instant pudding
 4 eggs
¾ cup oil
¾ cup Muscat À Deux
   Fresh Fruit
   Muscat À Deux Cream (recipe follows)

Place all ingredients in a mixing bowl, stirring for 5 minutes. Pour into greased bundt pan and bake in 350° oven for 45 to 50 minutes. Let set about 5 minutes before inverting pan to cool. Serve with fresh fruit and Muscat À Deux Cream.

Muscat À Deux Cream

 8 egg yolks
½ cup sugar
¾ cup Muscat À Deux
¼ cup Grand Marnier, Cointreau or Triple Sec
 1 cup cream, whipped

In top of doubleboiler, combine egg yolks, sugar, wine and liqueur. Set over boiling water and beat continuously for about 5 minutes or until mixture thickens. Remove from heat and whisk occasionally just until cool. Cover and refrigerate. When ready to serve, fold in whipped cream.

Zabaglione

Serves 4
Preparation Time: 10 Minutes

⅓ **cup Charles Krug Chenin Blanc or Muscat Canelli**
3 **Tbsps. Grand Marnier**
4 **egg yolks**

Combine the Chenin Blanc or Muscat Canelli and the Grand Marnier. Set aside.

In a double boiler over simmering water whip the egg yolks. Slowly add the wine mixture while stirring. The mixture will expand into a light creamy foam and will be done when it forms soft mounds. Do not overcook or the mixture will collapse.

Serve immediately in balloon type wine glasses or over fresh fruit.

DISCOVER THE WINE COUNTRY

*The following pages are a
guide to the secrets of
Napa and Sonoma counties.*

NAPA VALLEY WINES: A GLOBAL REPUTATION

WHILE THE NAPA VALLEY wine region is relatively small, it is studded with stars of the international wine world. Famed for its scenic vineyards, elegant wineries and delicious vintages, Napa Valley is blessed with consistent climate and favorable growing conditions.

Indeed, mention Napa Valley in most parts of the world and fine wine automatically comes to mind.

George Yount is credited with planting the first vines in Napa Valley. He had done some work for General Mariano Vallejo, who rewarded Yount with a large tract of land near present-day Yountville. By 1860, Yount managed to produce 5,000 gallons of wine per year.

And, of course, the Spanish padres planted grapes for wine at every Mission they founded in California.

BUT THE PATH of viticulture in California was changed forever by the arrival of European winemakers in the 1860s.

Charles Krug arrived from Prussia in 1858. For a time, he worked for Count Agoston Haraszthy, a Hungarian who became known as the father of California's viticulture. By 1861, Krug had established his own stone winery, which endures to this day.

In 1862, Jacob Schram cleared some mountainous land and began to plant the vines that formed Schramsberg, still a noted winery.

Pioneer winemakers at Beringer

THE BERINGER BROTHERS, Jacob and Frederick, foresaw the enormous potential of the Napa Valley. They hired Chinese laborers to dig out wine cellars in the soapstone hills and began making wine in 1876. In addition to a knowledge of Medoc-style winemaking, the Beringers introduced a lavish lifestyle. Frederick erected his stained-glass "Rhine House," a replica of the ancestral home in Germany.

Around this time, Haraszthy saw that the native American grapes were not on a par with the European versions. So, in 1861, he brought back 200,000 cuttings from Europe. These were planted throughout Napa and Sonoma counties.

In quick order, Georges De Latour founded Beaulieu Vineyards, Louis M. Martini established vineyards south of St. Helena, and the Christian Brothers set up a winery, novitiate and wine cellar.

Napa Valley wine had arrived in a big way, with 600 vineyards flourishing.

It was then that the first of the two great wine disasters struck.

The phylloxera vine beetle struck the vines in the 1870s, destroying the roots. Many vineyards were wiped out. But then somebody noticed that the American vines were not affected, just the European roots. The solution came when the premium European cuttings were grafted onto American root stock.

Within ten years, the vineyards were flourishing once again.

One postscript to the phylloxera story should be noted. The beetle infested the European vineyards in the 1880s. That's when the California wine industry came to the rescue, shipping thousands of phylloxera-resistant cuttings so that Europe could reestablish the wine industry there.

But the worst was yet to come: Prohibition.

FOR 14 YEARS—from 1919 to 1933—the manufacture, sale or transportation of any intoxicating liquor was forbidden. This simply devastated the Napa Valley. Vast acres of prime vineyards were ripped out to grow walnuts or prunes, or to be used as pasture land. A few wineries managed to survive via the loophole of making wine to be used in religious services.

Naturally, there was quite a bit of moonshining in the Napa Valley and some of the more remote wineries were able to continue producing wine in secret.

According to one story, moonshine was shipped to San Francisco through an ingenious ruse: the moonshine was loaded into caskets. The caskets, which sloshed when they were moved, were taken to Santa Rosa, where "mourners" would load them on a train bound for San Francisco. Nobody seemed to notice that the "mourners" always were the same men.

During Prohibition, many wineries fell into disrepair. Some were abandoned, some were sold and converted to other uses. These were bad days indeed for Napa Valley.

But eventually, Prohibition was repealed and—surprise of surprises—some well-aged wines were available from the clandestine remote wineries.

NONE OF THIS SEEMS possible now when you drive through the abundant Napa Valley. Hundreds of wineries are flourishing and the vineyards seem to go on forever. Nowadays, the wineries, with their posh estates, friendly tasting rooms and elegant restaurants are destinations of the first caliber.

Musical events such as the Charles Krug August Moon programs and the Robert Mondavi Summer Series attract music aficionados to days of good music in gorgeous surroundings.

And the keystone of it all are the fine wines of the Napa Valley— wines that surmounted many obstacles to become among the finest delights the world has to offer.

In order to help you focus on the best, we recommend the Napa Valley wineries on the following pages.

BEAULIEU VINEYARD

1960 St. Helena Highway
Rutherford, CA 94573
(707)963-2411
Route: Hwy. 29, 16 miles north of Napa
Open weekdays for tours and tasting 10AM–4PM
Weekends 10AM–5PM, retail sales

IT WAS IN 1900 that Georges de Latour settled in Rutherford, having come to California from his native France in search of fertile land to establish a vineyard and winery.

Monsieur de Latour brought with him a wealth of knowledge in viticulture and winemaking and a family name celebrated in both Bordeaux and Burgundy. In Rutherford, both climate and soil (today referred to as microclimate) met his most exacting demands. And so, Georges and Fernande de Latour built their home and called it "Beaulieu," beautiful place.

Today, at Beaulieu Vineyard, the best of the Old World and the New meld graciously to produce limited quantities of BV wines that are consistently excellent. They have been served for over half a century at official banquets honoring royal guests and heads of state, and are featured on the wine lists of the leading hotels, clubs and restaurants throughout the country.

Recipe: Risotto with Smoked Chicken & Walnuts, page 168

NAPA VALLEY'S LEGENDARY WINERY

215

BERINGER VINEYARDS

2000 Main Street
St. Helena, CA 94574
(707)963-7115
Open daily for tours and tasting 9:30AM–5PM
Retail sales

BERINGER VINEYARDS IS the oldest continuously operating winery in the Napa Valley, having received its bond in 1876. Nearly a century later, Beringer completely rebuilt its winemaking facilities so that it could crush, ferment and age small lots of wine separately and produce reserve and specific vineyard appellation wines.

The European quality standard that the Beringer brothers, Jacob and Frederick, brought to the wine industry were also applied to the elaborate construction of Frederick's 17 room home, the Rhine House. Inlaid wood floors, handcrafted wainscotting, coal burning fireplaces accented by imported tile and one of the largest collections of stained glass windows in Northern California characterize this historic house. Carefully maintained, the house now serves as a hospitality and tasting center for visitors to the winery.

Recipe: Duck Steak with Shallots, page 187

CAKEBREAD CELLARS

8300 St. Helena Highway
Rutherford, CA 94573
(707)963-5221
Route: East side of Hwy. 29
between Oakville and Rutherford
Tours and tasting by appointment
Retail sales daily 10AM–4PM

JACK AND DOLORES Cakebread's two favorite wines are Sauvignon Blanc and Cabernet Sauvignon, so it was no problem to choose which varieties to plant on their 60 acre ranch near Rutherford in 1972. It has worked out so well that they planted more Cabernet Sauvignon on their Hill Ranch, a grape's throw west toward the Mayacamas Mountains. Cakebread Cellars also buys Chardonnay from several vineyards in the Valley. The wines are made in a contemporary redwood winery, inspired by the barns that once dotted the Napa Valley countryside.

Jack and Dolores are joined in the family team by their two sons, Dennis and Bruce. The Cakebread philosophy of attention to details produces consistently well balanced, ageworthy wines.

Recipes: Spinach Balls with Sauvignon Blanc
    in Mustard Sauce, page 161
Warm Goat Cheese Salad
    with Golden Pepper Dressing, page 163
Grilled Rack of Lamb
    with Cabernet Lamb Sauce, page 172
Cherry & Chocolate Trifle, page 203

Cakebread Cellars

NAPA VALLEY

Cabernet Sauvignon

1987

CHIMNEY ROCK WINERY

5350 Silverado Trail
Napa, CA 94558
(707)257-2641
Route: 5 miles north of Napa
on the right side of Silverado Trail
Open daily for tasting 10AM–4PM
Tours by appointment
Retail sales

HACK AND STELLA Wilson laid the groundwork for Chimney Rock Winery in 1981 by planting 75 acres of estate vineyards in the Stag's Leap district. Specializing in premium quality estate-bottled Cabernet Sauvignon, Chardonnay and Fume Blanc, the winery name was inspired by a rocky crag on the eastern hills overlooking the vineyards.

In February, 1990, the distinctive Cape Dutch styled hospitality center was opened to the public. Nestled in a grove of poplar trees, the center serves as a focal point for corporate events, seminars, weddings and cooking schools.

Recipe: Mussels en Croute, page 192

CHRISTIAN BROTHERS-GREYSTONE

2555 Main Street
St. Helena, CA 94574
(707)963-0763
Route: North of St. Helena
Open daily for tours and tasting 10AM–4PM
Retail sales

GREYSTONE CELLARS IS the visitors' center of The Christian Brothers. Built in the late 1880's as a cooperative winery, the massive wine cellar served two purposes. It united small winegrowers and provided them with facilities to improve the quality of their wines; and it broke the merchants' deadlock on the growers by forcing them to buy higher quality wines at better prices.

In 1950, The Christian Brothers purchased Greystone Cellars outright with an immediate renovation to improve and modernize the then 60-year old building. In 1978, Greystone Cellars was placed in the National Register of Historic Places, in honor of its contributions to the California wine industry.

At The Christian Brothers, winemaking is an art blended with advanced technology. As the largest vineyard owner in the Napa Valley, The Christian Brothers have the resources to produce some of the finest wines in the region.

Recipe: Pears in Port Sauce, page 208

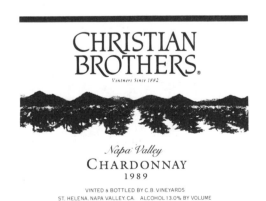

CUVAISON WINERY

4550 Silverado Trail
Calistoga, CA 94515
(707)942-6266
Route: 7 miles north of St. Helena
Open daily for tasting 10AM–5PM
Tours by appointment
Picnic facilities, retail sales

CUVAISON, FOUNDED IN 1969, has evolved through several changes into a highly focused small production winery, making a few varietals to world class standards for worldwide consumers.

Cuvaison's most significant change happened in 1979. That year, the Schmidheiny family of Switzerland acquired Cuvaison, then purchased 400 acres of vineyard land in the Carneros District of the Napa Valley. A planting program concentrating on Chardonnay followed. Varietals currently produced are Chardonnay, Cabernet Sauvignon, Merlot and Pinot Noir.

Recipe: Pasta with Shrimp in Lemon Butter Sauce, page 166

CUVAISON

DOMAINE CHANDON

1 California Drive
Yountville, CA 94599
(707)944-2280
Route: Hwy. 29 north of Napa in Yountville,
next to the Veterans Home.
Open daily for tours and tasting 11 AM–5PM
Retail sales

AFTER FOUR YEARS of development, Domaine Chandon opened in April, 1977, to offer its first sparkling wines, winery tour and champagne mini-museum. The winery was designed to reflect both Napa Valley and Champagne features, particularly the native stone walls and arched entries.

The sparkling wines which are the principal products of Domaine Chandon reveal their heritage: the Napa Valley winery has nearly unlimited access to the resources of its French parent company, Moët-Hennessy, Louis Vuitton.

Blending the classic Champagne varieties from select vineyards and different vintages give the cuvées their desirable complexity. It also allows a skillful blend that maintains a definite style and quality from year to year despite annual variation.

Recipes: Domaine Chandon Restaurant, page 32

FOLIE À DEUX WINERY

3070 St. Helena Highway
St. Helena, CA 94574
(707)963-1160
Route: 2 miles north of St. Helena on Hwy. 29
Open daily for tasting 11 AM–5 PM
Tours by appointment
Picnic facilities, retail sales

FOLIE À DEUX, a psychiatric diagnosis term, describes a "shared fantasy or delusion." Winery founders and mental health professionals, Evie and Larry Dizmang, feel that this name reflects their basic philosophy that the spirit of life and wine drinking should be festive and the two enjoyed together. A bottle of wine shared on a special occasion inspired a "folie" all its own and it is this celebrative spirit that they hope to capture in each of the wines. The theme is completed with an "inkblot" logo that invites your interpretation.

Founded in 1981, Folie à Deux sits atop a small knoll overlooking picturesque vineyards. The winery produces a wide range of exceptional wines: Chardonnay, Cabernet Sauvignon, Petite Sirah, Merlot, Zinfandel, Dry Chenin Blanc and a dry Muscat à Deux. The winery's latest "folie" is the Fantasie, a delicate Napa Valley Brut Champagne.

Recipe: Folie à Deux Wine Cake with Muscat Cream, page 209

FRANCISCAN VINEYARDS

1178 Galleron Road
Rutherford, CA 94574
(707)963-7111
Route: Hwy. 29, 3 miles south of St. Helena
Open daily for tours and tasting 10AM–5PM
Retail sales

THE FRANCISCAN OAKVILLE Estate is comprised of 240 acres in the Oakville district, bordered by the Napa River and Conn Creek in the heart of Napa Valley's premier growing region.

The climate and growing conditions of the Oakville district have proven themselves to be excellent for the production of Cabernet Sauvignon, Merlot, Zinfandel and Chardonnay. By pruning and thinning the vines regularly, the crop level is reduced to three to four tons per acre to achieve maximum intensity.

The winemaking philosophy at Franciscan Oakville Estate asserts that the quality and style of a wine is dictated by the vineyard. This method crafts wine of elegance, finesse and concentration.

Recipe: Grilled Salmon with Orange Saffron Butter, page 195

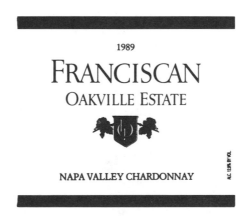

223

FREEMARK ABBEY WINERY

3022 St. Helena Hwy. North
St. Helena, CA 94574
(707)963-9694
Route Hwy. 29 and Lodi Lane
Open daily for tours and tasting 10AM–4:30PM
Retail sales

WINEMAKING AT FREEMARK Abbey dates from the autumn of 1886 when Josephine Tychson, the first woman in California to build a winery, began operating a winery on the site. Antonio Forni succeeded her and built the present stone structure before 1900. The Forni family continued operations until Prohibition. Following several ownerships, the winery was closed in the 1950's. In 1967, Freemark Abbey Winery was reactivated.

The annual production of 3,000 cases is primarily Chardonnay and Cabernet Sauvignon. Also produced is a small amount of Johannisberg Riesling which, when growing conditions permit, develops into Edelwein, a rich late-harvest wine with great depth and intensity.

The finest grapes from vineyards owned by grower-partners of the winery are hand-selected and hand-picked for Freemark Abbey wines. As a final pledge of excellence, the finished wines are held at the winery for optimum bottle aging to ensure superior quality and drinkability at release.

Recipe: Apricot Crown, page 200

FREEMARK ABBEY

1989
NAPA VALLEY
SWEET JOHANNISBERG RIESLING

Edelwein Gold

PRODUCED AND BOTTLED BY
FREEMARK ABBEY WINERY, ST. HELENA, CA., USA
ALCOHOL 9.2% BY VOLUME   RESIDUAL SUGAR 21.7%
HARVEST SUGAR 38.5° BRIX

GRGICH HILLS CELLAR

1829 St. Helena Hwy.
Rutherford, CA 94573
(707)963-2784
Open daily for tours and tasting 9:30AM–4:30PM
Retail sales

GRGICH HILLS CELLAR was formed in 1977 through the efforts of Miljenko Grgich and Austin Hills of the Hills Bros. coffee family. Grgich had the skill and expertise to make great wines and Hills, owner of established vineyards, had a background in business and finance.

The stellar attraction at Grgich Hills Cellar has been the Chardonnay. Grgich Chardonnays are rich and complex with the flowery aromas and intense fruitiness balanced by the wood of the French Limousin oak barrels. Also of interest is the elegant Fume Blanc produced from estate vineyards, cold-fermented and aged for five months in French oak barrels. As for the Zinfandels, the result has been rich and berry-like with impressive longevity.

Excellence is an uncompromising philosophy here. Never satisfied with yesterday's best, each vintage arrives as a new challenge to create the best wines of the future.

Recipe: Cheese Sticks, page 152

GRGICH HILLS

Napa Valley
CABERNET SAUVIGNON
1985
PRODUCED AND BOTTLED BY
GRGICH HILLS CELLAR, RUTHERFORD, CA
ALC. 13.3% BY VOL., CONTAINS SULFITES

HEITZ WINE CELLARS

436 St. Helena Highway So.
St. Helena, CA 94574
(707)963-3542
Open daily for tasting 11 AM–4:30PM
Tour by appointment weekdays
Retail sales

WHEN HEITZ WINE Cellars opened in 1961, the Napa Valley had fewer than 20 wineries. Today there are more than 200. The original winery on St. Helena Highway is still open to the public as a sales and tasting room for visitors and provides a glimpse into the origins of Heitz Cellars.

Within a few years, Heitz Cellars had outgrown the original premises and purchased the present 160-acre residence and ranch on Taplin Road. The home property was originally developed as a vineyard and winery in the 1880's by the Swiss-Italian family of Anton Rossi. The beautiful old stone cellar built in 1898 has made the transition through time and the Heitz family continues to mature fine wines within, carrying on the tradition of fine winemaking in the Napa Valley.

Growth has always been slow and calculated with quality and consistency of utmost importance. Today the winery accommodates an annual production of 40,000 cases with five family members overseeing a staff of eight.

Recipes: Apricot Prawns, page 190

1988
NAPA VALLEY
CHARDONNAY
ALCOHOL 13½% BY VOLUME
PRODUCED AND BOTTLED IN OUR CELLAR BY
HEITZ WINE CELLARS
ST. HELENA, CA, U.S.A. CONTAINS SULFITES

THE HESS COLLECTION WINERY

4411 Redwood Road
Napa, CA 94558
(707)255-1144
Route: Hwy. 29 north, exit left on Redwood,
8 miles to winery
Open daily for tours and tasting 10AM–4PM
Retail sales

IN 1978, WINERY owner Donald Hess acquired partially planted vineyard land high on the slopes of Mt. Veeder in California's Napa Valley. For over a decade, these rugged hillside vineyards have been developed and nurtured, proving exceptional grapes for the acclaimed wines of The Hess Collection. Cabernet Sauvignon and Chardonnay of singular quality are created by winemaker Randle Johnson.

The historic turn-of-the-century stone building which is home to The Hess Collection winery also contains a permanent exhibition of contemporary art. This internationally recognized collection of paintings and sculptures is open to the public.

Recipe: Bay Scallops with Spinach and Pernod, page 189

THE HESS
COLLECTION
NAPA VALLEY CHARDONNAY
1988
PRODUCED & BOTTLED BY THE HESS COLLECTION WINERY
NAPA, CALIFORNIA, USA
ALCOHOL 13% BY VOLUME

INGLENOOK-NAPA VALLEY

1991 St. Helena Highway
Rutherford, CA 94573
(707)967-3300
Open daily for tours and tasting 10AM–5PM

GUSTAVE NIEBAUM'S GOAL of "making the finest wines, to equal and excel the most famous vintages of France," set the standard for Inglenook-Napa Valley. The Finnish sea captain was fascinated by winemaking and dedicated his career to the art with his founding of Inglenook in 1879. An ambitious, energetic man, Niebaum imported cuttings from the finest vineyards in Europe and the wines they produced won numerous medals at international wine competitions.

Captain Niebaum made numerous trips to the commerce centers of Europe to expand his already considerable knowledge of wines, visiting the great vineyards and cellars.

Today, general manager and winemaker John Richburg, a U.C. Davis graduate, has been with Inglenook-Napa Valley since 1972 and continues the tradition of fine winemaking.

Recipe: Grilled Prawns with Tequila and
Nectarine Cream Sauce, page 191

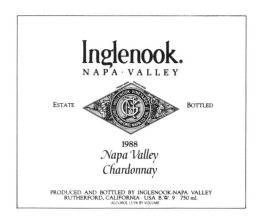

HANNS KORNELL
CHAMPAGNE CELLARS

1091 Larkmead Lane
Calistoga, CA 94574
(707)963-1237
Route: Hwy. 29, 4 miles north of St. Helena
Open daily for tours 10AM–4:30PM
Retail sales

HANNS KORNELL CHAMPAGNE Cellars in the Napa Valley represents four generations of dedication by the Kornell family. Their uncompromising ideals have built a reputation that is part of the legend of California winemaking.

In the early 1900's, the Kornell family was well known in the Rhine Valley of Germany for producing both still and sparkling wines. Their Schoenberger Kabinett was considered one of the best white wines in the world.

From his grandfather and uncle, Hanns Kornell learned the art and technical skill necessary to make great wines. Hanns lost virtually everything in the concentration camps of Nazi Germany and was left with little more than optimism and winemaking expertise when he was suddenly released in 1939. Thirteen years later, he realized his dream of adding the Kornell name to the winemaking history of California. He released his first bottle of California champagne in 1952.

Recipes: Barbecue Pork Tenderloin, page 175
Fresh Berries with Basil and Mint, page 201

750 ML (25.4 FL. OZ.)   H A N N S   ALCOHOL 12.0% BY VOL.

KORNELL

CALIFORNIA CHAMPAGNE   BRUT   METHODE CHAMPENOISE

CHARLES KRUG WINERY

2800 St. Helena Highway
St. Helena, CA 94574
(707)963-5057
Route: ¼ mile north of St. Helena on Hwy. 29
Open daily for tours and tasting 10 AM–4 PM

THE CHARLES KRUG Winery is the oldest winery in the Napa Valley. It was founded in 1861 by Charles Krug, a Prussian emigrant. The winery is presently owned by Peter Mondavi and Sons since 1943.

Charles Krug was a political theorist. Born in Trendelburg, Germany (then a part of Prussia) in 1825, he emigrated to the United States in 1847 to teach at the Free Thinkers' School in Philadelphia. A year later, joining the revolution that swept Europe, Krug wound up in a Prussian jail. When he was liberated, he returned to America where in 1860 he met Caroline Bale, a grandniece of General Mariano Vallejo. He planted a vineyard on her dowry in St. Helena and built the first winery in the Napa Valley.

Charles Krug was a pioneer in every sense of the word. He came to America at the age of 22 with nothing but will power and he helped found the wine industry we know today.

Recipe: Zabaglione, page 210

Charles Krug

NAPA VALLEY
MUSCAT CANELLI

Produced and Bottled by Charles Krug Winery
St. Helena, California   BW3110   Alcohol 9.5% by Volume

LOUIS M. MARTINI WINERY

254 St. Helena Hwy. South
St. Helena, CA 94574
(707)963-2736
Route: One mile south of St. Helena on Hwy. 29
Open daily for tours and tasting 10AM–4:30PM
Retail sales

DEDICATION TO FINE winemaking, reverence for the land and preservation of an innovative spirit—these are the principles underlying three generations of family ownership at the Louis M. Martini Winery.

Louis built the winery that bears his name in the Napa Valley in 1933. His state-of-the-art facility housed a cold fermentation room, an array of cooperage and an underground cellar. In addition, he had the foresight to purchase two of California's finest pre-Prohibition vineyards: La Loma in Carneros and Monte Rosso in Sonoma Valley.

When Louis's son, Louis P. Martini, became winemaker in 1954, he continued to build on his father's legacy. Today, Carolyn and Michael Martini, the third generation, are building on the tradition of Louis M. and Louis P., while placing their own stamp on this venerable Napa Valley winery.

Recipe: Spaghettini Primavera, page 169

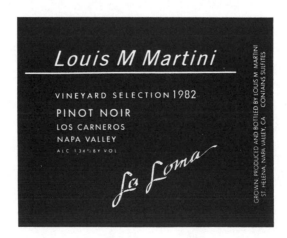

ROBERT MONDAVI WINERY

7801 St. Helena Hwy.
Oakville, CA 94562
(707)963-9611
Open for tours and tasting
May–October 9AM–5PM
November–April 10AM–4PM
Retail sales

SINCE FOUNDING THE Robert Mondavi Winery in California's renowned Napa Valley in 1966, Robert Mondavi's goals have remained constant: to produce world-class fine wines, to educate the American public about wine and its proper role as a mealtime beverage of moderation and to promote the gracious way of life, integrating wine with all fine arts.

Mondavi Winery has become internationally recognized as a symbol for great wine, comprehensive research and experimentation and diverse cultural events. The wines, now sold in more than 40 countries, consistently take top honors in international competitions.

Robert Mondavi, long an outspoken crusader for wine, is an industry leader with a reputation for risk-taking entrepreneurship. And although the Robert Mondavi Winery is just 25 years old, Robert's career spans more than 50 years of winegrowing in the Napa Valley.

With its welcoming arch and tower, the winery is known as a cultural center—the home of summer jazz concerts, classical concerts and drama, art exhibits, and a comprehensive food and wine program, including the well-known Great Chefs series.

Recipe: Chicken stuffed with Swiss Chard, page 183

1988
Napa Valley
CHARDONNAY
ALCOHOL 13% BY VOLUME

PRODUCED AND BOTTLED BY
ROBERT MONDAVI WINERY
OAKVILLE CALIFORNIA

Joseph Phelps Vineyards

200 Taplin Road
St. Helena, CA 94574
(707)963-2745
Tours and tasting by appointment
Retail sales daily 8AM–5PM

THE WINES OF Joseph Phelps Vineyards made their debut in the fall of 1974 with the release of the 1973 Johannisberg Riesling, one of California's first Germanic style wines. The winery and home vineyards are in Spring Valley, a small fold in the hills east of St. Helena long known as the Connolly Ranch.

In planting just 175 of the ranch's 670 acres to grapes, Phelps achieved the objective of preserving Spring Valley's natural appearance while matching a specific site with the individual needs of various varietals. In addition to its St. Helena area ranch, the winery owns a 50 acre "Region I" vineyard south of Yountville, a 30-acre plot of Cabernet Sauvignon in the Stag's Leap District, and has replanted to Cabernet Sauvignon, Merlot and Cabernet Franc 35 acres of vineyard land west of Rutherford. Most recently, a 55-acre parcel has been purchased in the Carneros District, the premium Chardonnay growing area of California, and 40 acres are currently being planted, with full production expected by 1994.

Recipe: Chevre Soufflé, page 153
Grilled Leeks with Mustard Cream, page 155
Grilled Pork Tenderloin, page 176
Black Currant Tea Ice Cream, page 202

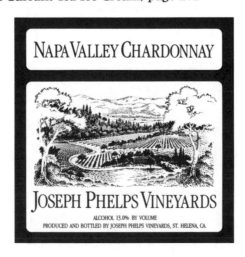

RUTHERFORD HILL WINERY

200 Rutherford Hill Road
Rutherford, CA 94573
(707)963-7194
Route: Off the Silverado Trail
Open daily for tours and tasting 10AM–4:30PM
Picnic facilities, retail sales

AT RUTHERFORD HILL, winemaking is both an art and a science. Rutherford Hill has blended traditional and innovative techniques in its quest to create wines that are at once complex and balanced, with the structure to age gracefully and yet be enjoyable upon release. The wines are given extended aging in small French oak barrels within Rutherford Hill's extensive hillside caves.

The wines are produced exclusively from select Napa Valley grapes, which form the foundation of the winery's reputation for consistent style and quality. These grapes come from a number of outstanding vineyards that are either owned by the winery or several of its partners or leased by the winery on a long-term basis.

Rutherford Hill Merlot, Cabernet Sauvignon, Chardonnay, Sauvignon Blanc, and Gewurztraminer are regularly honored with awards and critical acclaim. The winery also offers distinctive Exceptional Vineyards Selection (XVS) reserve wines, Library Reserve Cabernet Sauvignon and a limited production of vintage Zinfandel Port.

Recipe: Merlot Meat Loaf, page 174

RUTHERFORD HILL

Merlot

NAPA VALLEY

V. SATTUI WINERY

1111 White Lane
St. Helena, CA 94574
(707)963-7774
Open daily for tours and tasting 9AM–6PM
November–February 9AM–5PM
Picnic facilities and gourmet deli and cheese shop
Retail sales

IN 1882 VITTORIO SATTUI left Genoa, Italy, and sailed around The Horn to begin a new life in California. Of French-Italian heritage, he lost little time in doing what he loved best—making wines for his new friends and neighbors in the North Beach District of San Francisco. The demand for his wines grew. By 1885, V. Sattui Winery was officially established as a commercial venture. With the help of his wife and five children, the business flourished.

The Sattui reputation spread. The winery's label soon became a respected symbol of quality among fine California wines.

Recipe: Swordfish with Wild Mushrooms in Parchment, page 198

Est. 1885
of a total of 3,996 Bottles
1986
Preston Vineyards
NAPA VALLEY
Cabernet Sauvignon
PRODUCED AND BOTTLED BY
V. Sattui Winery
ST. HELENA, CALIFORNIA
ALCOHOL 13% BY VOLUME   CONTAINS SULFITES

Spring Mountain Vineyards

2805 Spring Mountain Road
St. Helena, CA 94574
(707)963-5233
Route: Left turn at second light onto St. Helena,
3 blocks then right on Spring Mountain.
Open daily for tasting 10AM–5PM
Retail sales, tours by appointment

SPRING MOUNTAIN VINEYARDS was founded in 1968 by Michael Robbins, a San Francisco businessman. The present property fulfills Robbins' vision of creating a true Chateau wine estate in the French tradition. The selection of Spring Mountain as the location for the filming of "Falcon Crest" is one testament to the success of this philosophy.

From its inception, Spring Mountain produced universally acclaimed wines. The winery currently produces Cabernet Sauvignon and Chardonnay. It formerly produced limited quantities of Sauvignon Blanc and Pinot Noir, some of which are currently available.

Recipe: Pork Chops and Apples, page 177

ST. SUPÉRY VINEYARDS & WINERY

8440 St. Helena Highway
Rutherford, CA 94573
(707)963-4507
Open daily for tours and tasting 9:30AM–4:30PM
Retail sales

ONE OF NAPA Valley's newest wineries, St. Supéry produces red and white wines from its extensive vineyard holdings.

A visit to St. Supéry provides a look at the future and the past, as well as an overview of the Napa Valley appellation and its importance in the world of wine. The historic house on the property has been fully restored and finished in the period as a "living museum" of viticultural life in the Napa Valley in the 1880's.

St. Supéry owners, the Skalli family of Paris, purchased the 1,500-acre Dollarhide Ranch in 1982 and began planting in 1983. The Dollarhide Ranch grapes have a distinctive character that form the backbone of St. Supéry's wine style.

Recipe: Leek & Potato Soup, with Avocado Cream, page 157

SUTTER HOME WINERY

277 St. Helena Highway South
St. Helena, CA 94574
(707)963-3104
Open daily for tasting 9AM–5PM
Retail sales, tours by appointment

THE HISTORY OF Sutter Home Winery dates back to 1874, when a Swiss-German immigrant named John Thomann established a small winery. Thomann died in 1900 and in 1906, his heirs sold the winery and the fine Victorian home Thomann had built beside it to another Swiss family, the Sutters. The winery and estate were rechristened Sutter Home.

Forty-one years later, Sutter Home was purchased by John and Mario Trinchero, Italian immigrant brothers whose family had long been active in the wine business.

Despite their humble beginnings, the Trincheros managed to transform Sutter Home during the 1980's into America's leading producer of premium varietal wines. Today, Bob Trinchero, his brother, Roger, and their sister, Vera, continue to operate Sutter Home according to the motto originated by their father and uncle: "A great product for a fair price."

Recipe: Salmon with Zinfandel Sauce, page 197

VICHON WINERY

1595 Oakville Grade
Oakville, CA 94562
(707)944-2811
Route: 1.5 miles west of Hwy. 29 on Oakville Grade
Open daily for tasting 10AM–4PM
Retail sales, tours by appointment

THE VICHON WINERY was founded in 1980 and purchased by the Robert Mondavi family in 1985.

The winery's limited production allows winemaker Michael Weis to taste each wine at each step in the winemaking process, blending the science of enology with the artistry in winemaking. The winery is dedicated to creating wines of great complexity, balance and longevity.

Vichon produces seven wines: Chevrignon (a proprietary blend of Sémillon and Sauvignon Blanc), Napa Valley Cabernet Sauvignon, Napa Valley Chardonnay, Napa Valley Merlot, Napa Valley Botrytis, Sémillon and Cabernet Blanc.

Recipe: Mushroom Strata, page 158

Sonoma County Wines: The Spice of Life

THE SONOMA COUNTY wine region, with its 150 wine-makers and 15 types of wine grapes, is the most diverse wine region in the United States.

The region is composed of five distinct wine-producing areas: the Sonoma Valley, Alexander Valley in the north, the Russian River Valley near Santa Rosa, part of Los Carneros district in the south and the Cazadero region near the ocean.

Because Sonoma County stretches from the fog-shrouded Pacific coast to sheltered valleys, to mountainous areas, so do its micro-climates and growing conditions. That's what makes Sonoma County so exciting for the wine lover: you never know what treasure you'll find next.

Most wine regions specialize in the better known wine varieties: Cabernet Sauvignon, Chardonnay or sparkling wines. In Sonoma County, you'll find those, but you'll also be able to compare a variety of Chenin Blancs, Fumé Blancs (also known as Sauvignon Blanc), Gewurztraminer, Johannisberg Riesling, Muscat, White Zinfandel, Gamay Beaujolais, Merlot, Petite Sirah and Zinfandel.

TWO FLAMBOYANT FIGURES started the wine industry in Sonoma County: Mexican General Mariano de Guadalupe Vallejo and Count Agoston Haraszthy.

Vallejo began making wine (relatively crude in nature) in Sonoma in the 1830s. In fact, the wily Vallejo tried to use wine as a weapon later on.

When the Bear Flag Revolt broke out on June 14, 1846, a group of American settlers captured the town of Sonoma and proclaimed California a republic.

240

Gundlach's Wine Vaults in San Francisco

THE REVOLUTIONARIES broke into Vallejo's home in order to arrest him. Vallejo invited the leaders into his home and gave them wine, the first intoxicant they had enjoyed in a long time. And, while they no doubt enjoyed the wine, they arrested him anyway.

The other Sonoma wine pioneer was Agoston Haraszthy, a one-time bodyguard of Emperor Ferdinand of Austria-Hungary, who fled his homeland after being marked for death following the revolution. Haraszthy came to America in search of a suitable vineyard site. He built the huge Buena Vista Winery outside Sonoma in 1857.

Vallejo and Haraszthy got involved in a friendly wine rivalry, trying to outdo one another in state and international competitions. That no doubt improved the quality of their wines.

Legend has it that the adventurous Haraszthy died in an alligator-infested river in Nicaragua in 1869.

SOME MADISON AVENUE marketing tactics linked Sonoma County wines with Napa Valley wines. As a result, some people still mistakenly link the two regions. In fact, the regions are separated by the Mayacamas Mountains and consist of very different microclimate regions. Napa Valley is entirely inland, while Sonoma County stretches from the ocean to the mountains and can support a wide variety of vineyards.

THE COOLER conditions of the Carneros district, the Russian River Valley, the Green Valley and the Cazadero region are well suited for Riesling, Gewurtztraminer, Pinot Noir and Chardonnay.

The warmer parts of the county—inland from the sea and north of San Pablo Bay—are well suited for Cabernet Sauvignon, Merlot and Sauvignon Blanc. The appellations to look for are Knights Valley, Chalk Hill, Dry Creek Valley and Alexander Valley.

The hottest regions—parts of Dry Creek Valley and Alexander Valley—are especially well suited for Zinfandel and Petite Sirah.

DON'T LET ALL these regions and wines confuse you or scare you off. Sonoma County is the land of opportunity for California wine lovers.

Sonoma County had only 20 wineries in 1973; today it has about 150. Magnificent wines abound throughout the region. Here's your chance to discover that little winery that can be your special find. To say nothing of relishing established wineries of great repute.

The following pages contain our recommendations from among the many fine wineries of Sonoma County.

242

BUENA VISTA WINERY & VINEYARDS

18000 Old Winery Road
Sonoma, CA 95476
(707)938-1266
Route: East on East Napa Street,
left on Old Winery Road
Open daily for tours and tasting
Picnic area, retail sales

FOUNDED IN 1857, Buena Vista Winery is widely known as the birthplace of the California wine industry. After a ten-year search for the perfect grape-growing area, Hungarian Count Agoston Haraszthy started this winery near the sleepy town of Sonoma. Shortly afterwards, he traveled to Europe, collecting grape cuttings from the world's great vineyards. In 1861, he returned to California with over 100,000 cuttings and planted California's first premium vineyards at Buena Vista.

A leisurely stroll down a wooded country lane leads to this State Historic Landmark. The impressive, ivy-covered stone winery buildings are tucked away in a secluded glen. Painstakingly restored ten years ago, the 1862 Press House is home to an art gallery, gift shop and tasting room. This historic winery also plays host to Summerfest, a series of weekend concerts and theatrical productions drawing guests from far and wide.

Recipe: Harvest Soup, page 156
Grilled Tarragon Chicken Skewers, page 185

CHALK HILL WINERY

10300 Chalk Hill Road
Healdsburg, CA 95448
(707)838-4306
Open Monday through Friday
Tours and tasting by appointment only

THE PHILOSOPHY OF Chalk Hill Winery is that great wines are born of a marriage between vineyard and winery. The grapes are grown on 286 acres of vineyard within the 1,100-acre Chalk Hill estate owned by Frederick P. Furth. The Chalk Hill region is primarily a hilly area and the grapes are grown at an elevation of between 200 and 600 feet. The soil, terrain and climate of this region are ideally suited for quality wine production.

The winery has recently been expanded to accommodate increased barrel aging and storage facilities. The estate grown wines produced at Chalk Hill Winery include Sauvignon Blanc, Cabernet Sauvignon and Chardonnay.

Recipes: Chicken with Tomatoes & White Wine Sauce, page 184
Mushroom Veal Stew, page 179
Pasta with Shrimp, Asparagus, Cream Sauce, page 166

CHATEAU SOUVERAIN

400 Souverain Road
Geyserville, CA 95441
(707)433-8281
Route: Highway 101 to Independence Lane Exit
Open daily for tours and tasting 10AM–4:30PM
Picnic area, retail sales

THE WINERY TRACES its ancestry to 1884, when Fulgenzio Rossini, a Swiss immigrant, claimed 160 acres of land under the Homestead Act. The land was located on Howell Mountain, just north of St. Helena.

In 1943, J. Leland Stewart, a retired businessman, purchased 60 acres of the Rossini property and settled down to the pleasure of raising fruit trees, nuts and grapes. In the following year, Lee decided he might try his hand at making just a little wine for his own use, and so Chateau Souverain was born. The name "Souverain" comes from the French word for "sovereign" and was inspired by Lee's young daughter, who was doing her French homework when asked by her father what a noble winery might be named.

After Lee sold the business in 1970, a facility in Sonoma County was a logical move. The winery, commanding one of Sonoma Valley's most panoramic views, overlooks the Alexander Valley, with the Mayacamas Mountains in the distance and 4,500-foot Mt. St. Helena clearly visible.

Recipe: Wild Rice Salad, page 164

CHATEAU ST. JEAN

8555 Sonoma Highway
Kenwood, CA 95452
(707)833-4134
Route: Highway 12 from Santa Rosa or Sonoma
Open daily for tours and tasting 10AM–4:30PM
Picnic facilities, retail sales

FOUNDED IN 1973 as a premium winery devoted to producing wines of uncompromising quality, Chateau St. Jean is home to critically acclaimed vineyard-designated Chardonnays and Fume Blancs, Cabernet Sauvignon and Johannisburg Riesling and Gewurztraminer in both dry and late harvest styles. The winery also established a reputation of quality for its sparkling wines.

Visitors to Northern California's wine country are consistently impressed by the charm and ambience of the 250-acre Chateau St. Jean estate. Its landscaped gardens, manicured lawns, 1920's era chateau and balconied tower command a presence unparalled among California wineries.

Wine sampling is enjoyed in style at Chateau St. Jean. The tasting room is located in the former living room of the chateau, while limited release wines are poured in the upstairs Vineyard Room. Picnics on the lawn surrounding the chateau, walks in the lovely gardens and self-guided tours of the winery allow visitors to sample the ambience of a world-class winery estate.

Recipe: Roasted Turkey with Herbed Pasta, page 170

Clos Du Bois

5 Fitch Street
Healdsburg, CA 95448
(707)433-5576
Route: Central Healdsburg off Highway 101
at Matheson and Fitch streets
Open daily for tasting 10AM–5PM
Retail sales, tours by appointment

WITH THE HARVEST of 1990, Clos Du Bois celebrated its 16th anniversary as a producer of premium California wines. Beginning with 2,000 cases in 1974, the winery will produce more than 250,000 cases this year and is still growing both in stature and size.

Clos du Bois today has 590 acres of planted vineyards in the Alexander Valley of Sonoma County, the most acreage of any wine producer in that appellation. Nearly 100 acres of vineyard in nearby Dry Creek Valley also contribute to the winery's production.

In California, Clos du Bois is the leader in the production of barrel-fermented Chardonnay. Other varietal wines produced are Sauvignon Blanc, Gewurztraminer, Cabernet Sauvignon, Merlot and Pinot Noir.

Recipe: Smoked Chicken Fettucine with Basil & Pinenuts, page 165

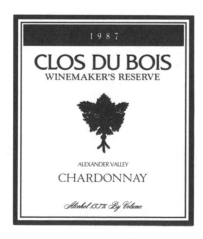

DE LOACH VINEYARDS

1791 Olivet Road
Santa Rosa, CA 95401
(707)526-9111
Route: 6 miles west of Santa Rosa off Guerneville Road
Open daily for tasting 10AM–4:30PM
Retail sales, tours by appointment
Picnic facilities

IN 1969 CECIL DE LOACH founded a 24-acre ranch on Olivet Road in the Russian River Valley. The land was owned by Louis Barbieri, whose father had planted Zinfandel grapes on the property between 1905 and 1927. Unable to entice his children to farm the vineyard, Barbieri began looking for a buyer who would. When he and Cecil De Loach met, the two men came to an agreement. Barbieri sold Cecil the land but continued to live in the farmhouse for a year so he could teach the De Loach family how to grow grapes.

In 1979 Cecil made 9,000 cases of wine, including Zinfandel, Pinot Noir, White Zinfandel and Gewurztraminer. In 1980 Cecil left the San Francisco Fire Department after 16 years of service. Devoting full time to this winery and vineyards, he was able to increase production to 12,000 cases and add Fume Blanc and Chardonnay to the line. In 1981 he made 18,000 cases of wine, including his first Cabernet Sauvignon. Today, the De Loach family's production is 75,000 cases.

Recipe: Chicken with Chardonnay and Caper Cream, page 181

248

FERRARI-CARANO VINEYARDS

8761 Dry Creek Road
Healdsburg, CA 95448
(707)433-6700
Route: Hwy. 101 north to Dry Creek Road, left, west 9 miles
Open daily for tasting 10AM–5PM
Retail sales, tours by appointment

THE FERRARI-CARANO vineyards and winery was founded in 1981 by Donald and Rhonda Carano. Named after Don's grandmother, Amelia Ferrari, the winery represents an old world heritage complemented by contemporary ideas and implementations.

The Caranos are both second-generation Italian-Americans strongly rooted in their Italian ancestry. Their families are native to the beautiful Liguria region of Italy and it was during his frequent childhood trips to his homeland that Don first became influenced by his grandfather's traditional winemaking practices.

The preparation of traditional Italian food is as integral a part of Don and Rhonda's heritage as the wine it so perfectly complements. Together, the Caranos create food and wine combinations that are long remembered.

Recipe: Veal Medallions on a Bed of Spinach
with Cabernet Sauvignon Sauce, page 180

1986
FERRARI·CARANO
ALEXANDER VALLEY
Cabernet Sauvignon
TABLE WINE

249

GLEN ELLEN WINERY

1883 London Ranch Road
Glen Ellen, CA 95442
(707)935-3000
Route: Jack London Park in Glen Ellen,
off Hwy. 12 north of Sonoma
Open daily 10AM–4:30PM
Tours and tasting
Picnic facilities, retail sales

THE BENZIGER FAMILY founded Glen Ellen Winery in 1980 after oldest son Mike found the ideal spot to make his dream of starting a vineyard and winery come true. A phone call to their home-town of White Plains, N.Y., was all it took for Mike's parents and six brothers and sisters to pull up stakes and move to California. They all pitched in to build the winery and replant the vineyards. Since 1982, more than 600 medals have been awarded to Glen Ellen wines at major wine competitions.

Visitors are welcome to enjoy Glen Ellen's manicured gardens and view the majestic hillside vineyards. Activities include picnics in the redwood grove, a self-guided tour and complimentary wine tasting.

Recipes: Goat Cheese Torta, page 154
Salmon in Champagne Cream Sauce
with Papaya, page 193
Orange Custard, Strawberries
& Muscat Canelli, page 207

GLORIA FERRER
CHAMPAGNE CAVES

23555 Highway 121
Sonoma, CA 95476
(707)996-7256
Route: 6.5 miles north
of Sears Point Raceway on Hwy. 121
Open daily for tours and tasting 10:30AM–5:30PM

GLORIA FERRER CHAMPAGNE CAVES is a young California winery with an old European heritage. The Ferrers have produced premium sparkling wines since the 13th century in Spain. The red-roof Catalonian-style winery in the hills of the Carneros district produces vintage and non-vintage Gloria Ferrer Brut.

The 30-minute tour includes walks through arched cellars, state-of-the-art winery complex, man-made caves, antique and modern equipment.

Recipe: Duck with Pear in Champagne, page 188

GRAND CRU VINEYARDS

1 Vintage Lane
Glen Ellen, CA 95442
(707)996-8100
Route: Hwy. 12 to Glen Ellen exit, turn right on Dunbar Road
Second tasting room: 8860 Sonoma Hwy. 12, Kenwood
Open daily for tasting 10AM–5PM
Tours by appointment
Picnic facilities, retail sales

LOCATED WELL OFF the beaten path in a tranquil setting of oak trees, Grand Cru's A-frame tasting room rests on some of the stone walls and concrete fermentation tanks that date back to the winery's early history in the mid-1880's when it was the Lemoine Winery. Some of the original vines surrounding the winery still produce grapes.

While sampling Grand Cru's fine wines, visitors to the tasting room enjoy a panoramic view of the Mayacamas Mountains that bend around the Valley of the Moon. Many take advantage of the picnic tables and barbecue pits nearby, complementing a bottle of Grand Cru wine with a picnic lunch.

Recipe: Mousse Grand Cru, page 206

GUNDLACH-BUNDSCHU WINERY

2000 Denmark Street
Sonoma, CA 95476
(707)938-5277
Route: East on Napa Rd., right on Eighth St. east,
left on Denmark to Sonoma Plaza
Open daily for tours and tasting 11AM–4:30PM
Picnic facilities, retail sales

JACOB GUNDLACH PLANTED 400 acres of vineyards and constructed a stone winery on an estate he called Rhinefarm in the Sonoma Valley. The first harvest took place in 1858 and marks the beginning of the Gundlach-Bundschu Winery.

In 1862, Charles Bundschu, a fellow Bavarian, became a partner when he married Gundlach's daughter. The partnership flourished and their wines became enormously popular, first in San Francisco, then on the East Coast. Before long, their warehouse covered an entire city block in San Francisco, and orders were filled for shipment throughout the world.

Disaster struck in 1906. The fire that swept through San Francisco after the earthquake totally destroyed Gundlach-Bundschu's warehouse and inventory. The winery survived this devastating setback and resumed making fine wines until shut down by the 13 years of Prohibition.

Today, Jim Bundschu, great-greatgrandson of Jacob Gundlach, continues with the proud tradition of making Gundlach-Bundschu wines.

Recipe: Chocolate Decadence Cake, page 204

HACIENDA WINERY

1000 Vineyard Lane
Sonoma, CA 95476
(707)938-3220
Open daily for tasting 10AM–5PM
Tours by appointment weekdays
Picnic area, retail sales

FOUNDED IN 1973, Hacienda Winery is located in the scenic Sonoma Valley, in the southern portion of Sonoma County. Constructed originally as a hospital in 1926, the winery is surrounded by the estate's historic vineyard, site of Count Agoston Haraszthy's first commercial vine plantings in 1857. Bordered on the south by the cool Carneros district, the estate vineyard, planted to Cabernet Sauvignon, Chardonnay, Merlot and Pinot Noir, produces fruit of intense flavor that typifies the wines of Hacienda Winery.

Currently producing 30,000 cases per year, Hacienda Winery is owned by the Cooley family and specializes in Chardonnay, Dry Chenin Blanc and Cabernet Sauvignon. Although production has grown each year in response to increasing sales, the winery remains committed to complete control of every aspect of fine wine production.

Recipe: Salmon & Sea Bass in Buerre Blanc Sauce, page 196

HACIENDA
1988 SONOMA COUNTY
Chardonnay
CLAIR de LUXE

PRODUCED AND BOTTLED BY HACIENDA WINERY
SONOMA, CALIFORNIA • B.W. 4623 • ALCOHOL 12.5% BY VOLUME

254

HOP KILN WINERY

6050 Westside Road
Healdsburg, CA 95448
(707)433-6491
Route: Hwy. 101 north, second Healdsburg exit,
left at Mill Street
Open daily for tasting 10AM–5PM
Tours by appointment
Picnic area, retail sales

A MAJESTIC OLD hops-drying barn now serves as home to Hop Kiln Winery, founded by Dr. Martin Griffin in 1975. The winery, a Russian River Valley landmark with its twin drying towers, is surrounded by 65 acres of old vineyard, which is part of the Griffin Sweetwater Springs Ranch.

Hop Kiln Winery produces eight varietal wines with an annual production of 8,000 cases. The emphasis is on small lots of carefully crafted wines.

Alongside the historic kiln are a charming pond and picnic area. An art gallery inside the winery displays local artists' work.

Recipe: Lamb with Oyster Mushroom Ragout, page 173

KENWOOD VINEYARDS

9592 Sonoma Highway
Kenwood, CA 95452
(707)833-5891
Open Monday through Friday for tasting 10AM–4:30PM
Retail sales, tours by appointment

KENWOOD VINEYARDS WAS founded in 1970, when six wine enthusiasts from the San Francisco Bay Area acquired the historic Pagani Brothers winery in Kenwood. The winery continues to be housed in the original Sonoma barn buildings.

The harvest from each vineyard is handled separately within the winery to preserve its individuality. Such "small lot" winemaking allows the winemaker to bring each lot of wine to its fullest potential, as shown in Kenwood's "Jack London Ranch" and "Beltane Ranch" bottlings. A blend of the finest barrels of Cabernet Sauvignon from each vintage, the "Artist Series," also reveals the rewards of this dedication to excellence.

Recipe: Prosciutto Wild Mushroom Bread, page 160

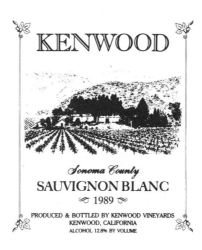

KENWOOD

Sonoma County
SAUVIGNON BLANC
1989

PRODUCED & BOTTLED BY KENWOOD VINEYARDS
KENWOOD, CALIFORNIA
ALCOHOL 12.8% BY VOLUME

KORBEL CHAMPAGNE CELLARS

13250 River Road
Guerneville, CA 95446
(707)887-2294
Route: Hwy. 101 to River Road, west 12 miles
Open daily for tours and tasting 10AM–3:30PM
Retail sales 9AM–5PM

KORBEL CHAMPAGNE CELLARS, the nation's oldest producer of "methode champenoise" champagne, has long been recognized as an important California winery.

The Korbel brothers originally settled in Northern California to establish a cigar box factory using the huge redwood trees. After clearing the redwoods, they discovered that they were owners of prime farmland and began planting grapevines among the redwood stumps. Company records document the first shipment of Korbel Champagne in the spring of 1882.

Korbel Champagne Cellars today is still very much a family business. The traditions and champagne-making philosophy of Korbel have remained virtually unchanged over the years.

Recipe: Barbecued Chicken Salad, page 151

MARK WEST VINEYARDS

7000 Trenton-Healdsburg Rd.
Forestville, CA 95436
(707)544-4813
Route: Hwy. 101 north, exit Sonoma/Sebastopol
Open daily for tasting 10AM–5PM
Tours by appointment
Picnic area, retail sales

OVERLOOKING THE MARK West Creek, the vineyards are cradled by the Mayacamas Mountains to the east, and the Pacific Ocean to the west in a valley of rolling hills and micro-climates, characteristics well suited to the Pinot Noir, Chardonnay and Gewurztraminer varietals. Named after British adventurer Marcus West, the vineyards encompass 116 acres.

Proprietors Bob and Joan Ellis established the vineyards in 1974. Their new adventure quickly resulted in award-winning estate wines appreciated by connoisseurs the world over. Mark West wines attract serious devotees, establishing a niche for the vineyards among the more sophisticated selections of California wines.

Recipe: Chicken Florentine, page 182

Matanzas Creek Winery

6097 Bennett Valley Road
Santa Rosa, CA 95404
(707)528-6464
Route: Sebastopol, Bennett Valley
Monday–Saturday tours and tasting 10AM–4PM
Sunday Noon–4PM
Retail sales

SINCE ITS FOUNDING in 1978, Matanzas Creek Winery has distinguished itself as one of California's premium estates, producing wines of consistent excellence. Such success has not been accidental.

From the outset, owners Sandra and Bill MacIver intended to create the best wine possible. They chose only the finest grapes from the more desirable cooler climates and built a winemaking philosophy that fused traditional handcrafting with modern technology. This devotion to superior quality has assured their wines a place at the top of five-star wine lists both in the U.S. and abroad and has won them critical acclaim, vintage after vintage.

Current total production is 30,000 cases. Since the guiding philosophy at the winery has always been quality before quantity, output will remain at least at that level through 1992. Wines produced are Sonoma County Chardonnay, Sonoma County Sauvignon Blanc and Sonoma County Merlot.

Recipe: Baked Salmon with Garlic, Basil & Tomatoes, page 194

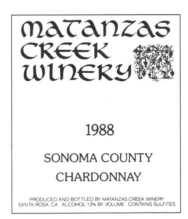

MATANZAS
CREEK
WINERY

1988

SONOMA COUNTY
CHARDONNAY

PRODUCED AND BOTTLED BY MATANZAS CREEK WINERY
SANTA ROSA CA ALCOHOL 13% BY VOLUME CONTAINS SULFITES

MURPHY-GOODE ESTATE WINERY

4001 Highway 128
Geyserville, CA 95441
(707)431-7644
Route: From Alexander Valley Rd. north on Hwy 128
Open daily for tasting 10AM–5PM
Retail sales, tours by appointment

UNTIL SIX YEARS ago, the land on which Murphy-Goode is located was mostly planted to prune orchards. In 1979, long-time Alexander Valley growers Tim Murphy and Dale Goode formed a partnership to plant Murphy-Goode vineyards.

Committed to producing the finest grapes possible, Murphy and Goode set out a vineyard with choice varieties and clonal selections, featuring the most modern technological farming practices in the industry. The irrigation system is one of the most expensive per acre in any vineyard. It has overhead sprinklers for frost protection in spring and underground drip for water management during the growing season. To hear Murphy and Goode talk about drip emitters and neutron probes, it sounds more like Star Wars than farming.

Murphy-Goode Estate Vineyards grows a variety of premium winegrapes, concentrating on Fume (Sauvignon) Blanc, Chardonnay, Merlot and Cabernet Sauvignon.

Recipe: Thai Grilled Chicken, page 186

260

SEBASTIANI VINEYARDS

389 Fourth Street East
Sonoma, CA 95476
(707)938-5532
Daily tours and tasting 10AM–5PM
Retail sales

SEBASTIANI VINEYARDS HAS a particularly proud heritage, for it has a double heritage. Its original vineyard, adjacent to its binning cellars, was founded in 1825 by Franciscan padres who made altar wines for the Mission de Sonoma.

Fifty years later in the Tuscany region of Northern Italy, Samuele Sebastiani began learning the techniques of tending noble vines and the art of making fine wines. He immigrated to American in 1895 with the dream of starting his own winery. By 1904, Samuele purchased the winery's present stone cellars and soon earned a reputation for producing distinctive wines with the character of the Old World.

August Sebastiani inherited the winery upon his father's death in 1944. It was he who began bottling wine under the family name and brought the wines to international acclaim. Under the direction of winery matriarch Sylvia Sebastiani, the third generation is continuing the Sebastiani tradition of excellence.

Recipe: Italian Biscotti, page 205

A Sebastiani Family
Selection

1987

SEBASTIANI

CABERNET SAUVIGNON
SONOMA COUNTY, CALIFORNIA

75 cl   Alc 12.5% Vol.

PRODUCED AND BOTTLED BY SEBASTIANI VINEYARDS, SONOMA, CA U.S.A. PRODUCE OF THE U.S.A.

SIMI WINERY

16275 Healdsburg Ave.
Healdsburg, CA 95448
(707)433-6981
Route: Hwy 101 north to Dry Creek Rd. exit,
left on Healdsburg Ave.
Open daily for tours and tasting 10AM–4:30PM
Picnic facilities, retail sales

SIMI WINERY WAS founded in 1876 by two brothers, Guiseppe and Pietro Simi, who emigrated from the Tuscan region of Italy. Family owned until 1971, Simi is now owned by Moet-Hennessy/ Louis Vuitton, a prestigious French producer of luxury goods.

Simi is noted for its Chardonnay, Cabernet Sauvignon and Sauvignon Blanc. Its wine style emphasizes balance, elegance, power and complexity.

Recipe: Tuna with Lavender, page 199

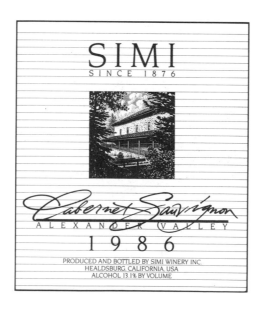

ST. FRANCIS WINERY

8450 Sonoma Highway
Kenwood, CA 95452
(707)833-4666
Route: Hwy. 12 southeast from Santa Rosa
northwest from Sonoma
Open daily for tasting 10AM–4:30PM
Tours by appointment
Picnic facilities, retail sales

JOE MARTIN TURNED from white-collar executive to vine-grower in 1971 with his acquisition of what is currently the St. Francis estate. His discriminating search for the ideal site ended with the purchase of an exquisite 100-acre property. For eight years he produced and sold his grapes to neighboring wineries. After having built an exceptional reputation for his grapes, especially his Merlot and Chardonnay, Joe Martin decided to build his own winery.

In 1979, the St. Francis winery was completed and christened after Saint Francis of Assisi. This rustic winery was built to a 40,000-case capacity. The property is currently apportioned 30% to Chardonnay and 70% to Merlot grapes which are used for the production of St. Francis' two estate wines.

Recipe: Barbecued Leg of Lamb, page 171

1988
ST. FRANCIS
ESTATE BOTTLED
SONOMA VALLEY
MERLOT

A KOBRAND CORPORATION CALIFORNIA SELECTION

VIANSA WINERY

25200 Arnold Drive
Sonoma, CA 95476
(707)935-4700
Route: Hwy 121, 4 miles north of Hwy 37 junction
Open daily for tours and tasting 10AM–5PM
Picnic facilities, retail sales

NESTLED IN THE rolling hills of Sonoma Valley and surrounded by a vineyard, an olive grove and vegetable garden, lies Viansa Winery and Italian Marketplace. Visitors can tour the old-world Tuscan-styled winery, enjoy the aromas of aging Cabernet Sauvignon in the vaulted cellar and experience the finest wines and foods in wine country.

Viansa wines reflect three generations of expertise in exceptional winemaking. The style combines the intensity and structure of Napa grapes with the subtleties and fruit character of Sonoma grapes. The resulting wines have an extended range of flavors.

From Viansa's Italian Marketplace, visitors may also enjoy a savory selection of gourmet picnic foods. The recipes are unique and developed by owner Vicki Sebastiani in her "Cal-Ital" style, a blend of California and Italian ingredients and flavors.

Recipe: Torta Rustica, page 162

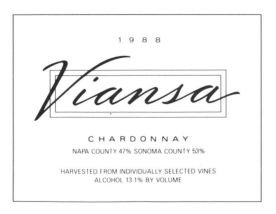

1 9 8 8

CHARDONNAY
NAPA COUNTY 47% SONOMA COUNTY 53%

HARVESTED FROM INDIVIDUALLY SELECTED VINES
ALCOHOL 13.1% BY VOLUME

WILLIAM WHEELER WINERY

130 Plaza Street
Healdsburg, CA 95448
(707)433-8786
Route: ½ block off the Plaza Center
Open daily for tasting 11AM–4PM
Retail sales

BILL AND INGRID Wheeler purchased a 175-acre ranch nestled in the rolling hills of Dry Creek Valley in 1970 with the dream of growing fine wine grapes. The land was right, beautiful hillsides and benchlands with fast draining shallow soils to challenge the vines. Old vines and orchards were replaced by carefully selected clones of varieties chosen for the particular soil and climate. Where the vines must struggle, they produce small grapes with concentrated flavors and wines of distinction.

The Wheelers then purchased and renovated a building off the downtown plaza in Healdsburg. Uniquely located, this discreet facility contains a tasting room and aging cellar with over 300 small French oak barrels. Their second winery, built later the same year for crushing, pressing and fermentation, is located at the vineyard, 800 feet above the valley floor.

Recipe: Mustard Pepper Steak, page 178

HOW YOU CAN MEASURE UP...

LIQUID MEASURES

1 dash	6 drops
1 teaspoon (tsp.)	⅓ tablespoon
1 tablespoon (Tbsp.)	3 teaspoons
1 tablespoon	½ fluid ounce
1 fluid ounce	2 tablespoons
1 cup	½ pint
1 cup	16 tablespoons
1 cup	8 fluid ounces
1 pint	2 cups
1 pint	16 fluid ounces

DRY MEASURES

1 dash	less than ⅛ teaspoon
1 teaspoon	⅓ tablespoon
1 tablespoon	3 teaspoons
¼ cup	4 tablespoons
⅓ cup	5 tablespoons plus 1 teaspoon
½ cup	8 tablespoons
⅔ cup	10 teaspoons plus 2 teaspoons
¾ cup	12 tablespoons
1 cup	16 tablespoons

VEGETABLES AND FRUITS

Apple (1 medium)	1 cup chopped
Avocado (1 medium)	1 cup mashed
Broccoli (1 stalk)	2 cups florets
Cabbage (1 large)	10 cups, chopped
Carrots (1 medium)	½ cup, diced
Celery (3 stalks)	1 cup, diced
Eggplant (1 medium)	4 cups, cubed
Lemon (1 medium)	2 tablespoons juice
Onion (1 medium)	1 cup, diced
Orange (1 medium)	½ cup juice
Parsley (1 bunch)	3 cups, chopped
Spinach (fresh) 12 cups, loosely packed	1 cup cooked
Tomato (1 medium)	¾ cup, diced
Zucchini (1 medium)	2 cups, diced

RECIPE INDEX

Warm scallops, lemon coriander
  vinaigrette, 67
Warm winter greens with
  pancetta, 117
Wild rice, 164

Sauces:
Basil, 64
Lasagne, 57
Pesto, 86
Red bell pepper, 78
Wasabi butter, 88

Soups:
Anise, cream of, 129
Arugula, cream of, 96
Avocado, chilled, 39

Chicken coconut, 53
Eggplant roasted, red onion, 107
Eggplant, Japanese, 34
Harvest, 156
Leek & potato, avocado cream, 157
Pumpkin with minted cream, 21
Pumpkin, blue cheese, chives, 137
Seafood brodetto, 73
Squash, spicy, 25

Vegetables and Side Dishes:
Eggplant, gingcr butter, 44
Leeks grilled, mustard cream, 155
Mushroom strata, 158
Polenta, red bell pepper sauce, 78
Polenta grilled with jack
  cheese, 118

ABOUT THE AUTHOR

KATHLEEN DEVANNA FISH, a native of California, has lived in Monterey for the past twelve years.

Her experience as owner-operator of three businesses in the travel and hospitality industry has been invaluable in coordinating the material for "California Wine Country Secrets" and her other books, "San Francisco's Secrets" and "Monterey's Secrets".

A gourmet cook, Kathleen is always looking for creative recipes that have style and character.

She lives with husband, Robert, and their dog, Dreamer, on a boat in Monterey harbor.

The Marketing Arm
P.O. Box 1994
Monterey, CA 93942
408-373-0592

Please send _____ copies of California Wine Country Secrets of Napa Sonoma at $12.95 each.

Please send _____ copies of San Francisco's Secrets at $12.95 each.

Please send _____ copies of Monterey's Secrets at $12.95 each.

Add $2.00 postage and handling for the first book ordered and $1.25 for each additional book. Please add 6½% sales tax for books shipped to California addresses.

Please charge my ☐ Visa ☐ MasterCard # _____

Expiration Date _____ Signature _____

Enclosed is my check for _____

Name _____

Address _____

City _____ State _____ Zip _____

☐ This is a gift. Send directly to:

Name _____

Address _____

City _____ State _____ Zip _____

☐ Autographed by the author.

Autographed to _____

271